English World

Workbook 7 A2+

Mary Bowen, Liz Hocking and Wendy Wren

Macmillan Education Limited
4 Crinan Street
London N1 9XW
Companies and representatives throughout the world

ISBN: 978-0-230-03260-6

Text © Mary Bowen, Liz Hocking, Wendy Wren 2012

Design and illustration © Macmillan Education Limited 2012

First published 2012

All rights reserved; no part of this publication may be reproduced, stored in a retrieval system, transmitted in any form, or by any means, electronic, mechanical, photocopying, recording, or otherwise, without the prior written permission of the publishers.

Concept design by Anna Stasinska
Page design, layout and art editing by Wild Apple Design Ltd.
Illustrated by Kathryn Baker (Sylvie Poggio) pp41, 95, 97. Martin Bustamante (Advocate) pp22, 23, 27, 76t, 77. Peter Dobbin (Pickled Ink) pp15, 48, 49, 51, 53, 89. Anna Hancock (Beehive) p8 and character heads throughout. Niall Harding (Beehive) pp7, 30, 33, 38, 76b, 80, 82, 86, 87, 105, 107, 108. Kate Rochester (Pickled Ink) pp58, 59, 60, 63, 96, 99.
Cover design by Oliver Design
Cover credit: Alamy/James Ingram (cl), Alamy/Maximillian Weinzierl (tr); Corbis Steve Hix/Somos Images (tl); FLPA/Mark Newman (b); Getty (cr).

The publishers would like to thank the Macmillan teams around the world and Hala Fouad, Hoda Garraya, Caroline Toubia, Samira Mahameh, Adnan Bazbaz, Nisreen Attiya, Mohammed Abu Wafa, Fatima Saleh, Muna Ghazi, Anna Solovyeva, Tatyana Olshevskaya, Irina Shikyants, Irina Burdun, Elena Mitronova, Inna Daugavet, Olga Pavlenko, Svetlana Potanina, Irina Ostrovskaya, Zhanna Suvorova, Sergey Kozlov, Olga Matsuk, Elena Gordeeva and Marina Kuznetsova.

The authors and publishers would like to thank the following for permission to reproduce their photographs: Commissioned images by Lisa Payne pp9,10, 18, 28, 36, 46, 54, 64, 72, 82, 90, 100, 108.

These materials may contain links for third party websites. We have no control over, and are not responsible for, the contents of such third party websites. Please use care when accessing them.

Although we have tried to trace and contact copyright holders before publication, in some cases this has not been possible. If contacted we will be pleased to rectify any errors or omissions at the earliest opportunity.

Printed and bound in China
2023 2022 2021 2020
20 19 18

Contents

Unit 1 Magazines — page 4

Unit 2 City life — page 12

Revision 1 — page 20

Unit 3 Life at the edge — page 22

Unit 4 Advertisements — page 30

Revision 2 — page 38

Unit 5 Great lives — page 40

Unit 6 What a character! — page 48

Revision 3 — page 56

Unit 7 This is what to do — page 58

Unit 8 A point of view — page 66

Revision 4 — page 74

Unit 9 How the body works — page 76

Unit 10 Later that day ... — page 84

Revision 5 — page 92

Unit 11 Sports reports — page 94

Unit 12 On stage — page 102

Revision 6 — page 110

Grammar reference — page 112

Irregular verb list — page 120

Word list — page 122

Conversational words and phrases — page 126

1 Magazines

Reading comprehension

1 Read The *portrait* project again.

2 Write T (true) or F (false).
1. The *Portrait* project brings together Art and Technology. __T__
2. Professor John Brown is running Hampton University. __F__
3. In the project, students create a portrait of the place where they go to school. __F__
4. Professor Brown told the students that they must decide what to tell people. __T__
5. After the first session the students rushed for the door. __F__
6. In the second session Professor Brown talked about producing the portrait. __T__
7. The students had to choose who they wanted to work with. __T__
8. Professor Brown put up message boards to help students find each other. __T__

3 Correct the false statements.
John Brown is running the project.
Creating a portrait of our town.
rush for the leaflets.

4 Answer the questions about the interview with Laura. Write short answers.
1. How often are the students going to meet? every week
2. What three things is Laura interested in? photography   film   computers
3. What does Laura do every Monday? computer club
4. What films does she like? Cartoon films and surfing the internet
5. Where does she not like going? going to the dentis much

5 Write the name of the person who …
1. told the students about the project __Ross__
2. was interviewed by Patsy __Laura__
3. is interested in people __Patsy__
4. works at Hampton University __Holly__
5. is interested in photography __Laura__
6. likes making new friends __Laura__

6 Write the names of the two people who …
1. reported the project __Laura__ _____
2. don't like the dentist __Laura__ _____
3. chatted to Patsy __Laura__ _____
4. go to West Hill Academy _____ _____

Vocabulary

1 Some words have more than one meaning. Read the sentence below then circle the correct meaning (a, b or c) for *running*.

Professor Brown is <u>running</u> the project.

a flowing
(b) organising
c going fast by taking steps quickly

> If the meaning you know doesn't make sense, check for a new meaning.

2 Write the correct definition from Exercise 1 for *running* in these sentences.
1 Tears were running down the girl's face. _flowing_
2 The children were running across the playground. _going fast by taking steps quickly_

3 Write the correct definition for *present* next to each sentence.

| present adj. here | present n. gift | present n. this time, now | present v. show |

1 We gave Grandma a present on her birthday. _gift_
2 Sam did not present his project today because he was ill. _show_
3 Ben was not present for the exam because he was ill. _here_
4 In the past, people travelled by horse but in the present, they use cars. _this, time, now_

4 Read each sentence in Exercise 3. Circle *present* in the sentence where it is pronounced differently.

5 Write the correct meaning of *get on* next to each sentence.
1 We must **get on** the train now because it will leave in a minute. _____
2 Anna and Lily often play together and they **get on** very well. _____
3 Sam is **getting on** well with his project – it's going to be good! _____

6 Match the verbs from the text with the verb that has a similar meaning.

| find out | report | respond | invite | create |

1 ask _____
2 make _____
3 discover _____
4 tell _____
5 reply _____

> Use your dictionary to help you.

7 Choose three of the words from the box and use them in sentences of your own.

_____
_____
_____

Unit 1 Vocabulary: words with more than one meaning; synonyms 5

Working with words

1 Write the words next to the correct definition.

volunteer   present   portrait   session   include   decide   get on

1. **portrait** — a drawn or painted picture of a person
2. **volunteer** — a person who offers to do something without payment
3. **session** — a period of time in which an activity is done
4. **decide** — to think about something and then choose what to do
5. **present** — to show
6. **include** — to put something with other things
7. **get on** — to enjoy being with somebody

2 Read these verbs. Use the suffix -tion or -ment to make a noun. Write the noun. Think about the changes you need to make to the root word before you add the suffix.

1. equip**ment**
2. invit**ation**
3. present**ation**
4. imagin**ation**
5. argu**ment**
6. animate **animation**

3 Complete the sentences with the words in Exercise 2.

1. Our cousin has sent us an **invitation** to her wedding.
2. My uncle is an artist who works in film **animation**.
3. When you write a story, use your **imagination** to help you think of ideas.
4. My brothers had a big **argument** about their new computer game.
5. Make sure you have the right **equipment** when you go skiing.
6. All our parents came for the **presentation** of the class prizes.

4 abc Spelling: complete the words. Write ss or sh.

1. mi**ss**ion
2. fa**sh**ion
3. cu**sh**ion
4. discu**ss**ion
5. impre**ss**ion
6. ru**sh**ing
7. Ru**ss**ian
8. bru**sh**es

5 abc Write the words in Exercise 4 next to the correct definition. Check your spelling.

1. a soft object for sitting on or putting on a chair or sofa **cushion**
2. objects used to clean teeth or tidy hair **brushes**
3. a talk between two or more people **discussion**
4. hurrying **rushing**
5. a person from Russia **Russian**
6. a style, especially in clothing **fashion**
7. a task done by an individual or group **mission**
8. the mark left on something by pressing on it **impression**

Grammar

1 Look at the picture and complete the sentences. Use the verbs in the box. Use the present continuous.

| make | report | smile | hold | interview | record |

1. Patsy Parker _____ some footballers.
2. _____ she _____ notes?
3. She _____ the interview.
4. The footballers _____ happily.
5. They _____ a cup.
6. Will Jones _____ not _____ on the match.

2 Complete the sentences with the verbs in the box. Use the present simple.

| go | wear | meet |
| live | work | teach |

1. Will and Patsy _____ for a magazine.
2. _____ they often _____ interesting people?
3. Patsy always _____ smart clothes to work.
4. Professor Brown _____ at the university.
5. Laura _____ not _____ to the same school as Holly.
6. Ross and Jack _____ not _____ in the same part of town.

3 Complete the sentences with the verbs in brackets. Use the present simple or the present continuous.

1. Today the students _____ about The *portrait* project. (learn)
2. Be quiet! I _____ to do my homework. (try)
3. Holly often _____ shopping with her mother. (go)
4. The children _____ not usually _____ to reporters. (speak)
5. The score is 3–1. Our team _____! (win)
6. _____ Ross _____ doing puzzles and quizzes? (enjoy)

4 Remember!

> We usually use the long forms of verbs when we are writing.

> We usually use the short forms of verbs when we are speaking.

Write the long forms of the verbs.

1. I'm reading. *I am reading.*
2. She's a student. _____
3. You're late. _____
4. He doesn't play. _____

Write the short forms of the verbs.

5. We are waiting. *We're waiting.*
6. They do not swim. _____
7. I am studying. _____
8. We do not understand. _____

Unit 1 Grammar: present simple; present continuous; long and short forms

Grammar in use

1 Complete the sentences with the verbs in the box.
Use the present simple.

| ~~think~~ | ~~cost~~ | ~~understand~~ | ~~include~~ | ~~remember~~ | ~~sound~~ |

1 John's teacher __thinks__ he will pass his exam.
2 I __can__ not __remember__ the professor's name.
3 This new computer game __sounds__ fun.
4 The film __includes__ some amazing special effects.
5 How much __does__ that CD __cost__?
6 Lucy __understands__ Spanish but she can't speak it.

2 Read.

> When **have** means **own** or **hold**, we use the present simple.

> I have got a cat.
> I haven't got a dog.
> Have you got a pet?

> I have a cat.
> I don't have a dog.
> Do you have a pet?

> With **got** or not with **got**?
> That is the question!

> **got** is used in British English.

3 Complete the sentences. Use *have*.

1 Polly and Pete __have__ got lots of pets. Polly __has__ got three cats and Pete __has__ got two dogs. They __have__ not got one parrot. They __have__ got four! __Have__ you got any pets?
2 Mandy and Andy __have__ black hair. Mandy __has__ brown eyes. __Has__ Andy __has__ brown eyes, too? No, Andy __does__ not __have__ brown eyes. He __has__ blue eyes. What colour eyes __do__ you __have__?

4 Complete the sentences with words from the boxes.

| do | make | | a decision | a project | a list | homework | friends |

1 Ben is going shopping but he is very forgetful. He must __make a list__.
2 The teenagers are going to __do project__ about their town.
3 You will like your new school. You will soon __make friends__.
4 Are we going to the mountains or the seaside? We must __make a decision__.
5 If Milly __does__ her __homework__ now, she can watch TV later.

Individual writing: writing an interview

You have read **an interview** between Patsy and Laura.
You have written **an interview** between Patsy and Holly.
Now write **an interview** between Patsy and Ross.

Read Student's Book page 14 again.
It tells you how to write an **interview**.

Read Ross's personal profile.

name:	Ross
age:	14
lives in:	North Park
brother:	Harry, aged 16
sister:	Amy, aged 10
school:	North Park College
interests/hobbies:	art, swimming, basketball
likes:	animals (all animals but particularly my cat, Claws)
dislikes:	zoos, people who are cruel to animals

Think about the questions Patsy can ask.

- Remember the question words:

   What …?   When …?   Where …?   Which …?   Who …?   How …?

- Try to write the interview without looking back at the questions you wrote on Student's Book page 14.

Use the information in the profile to write Ross's answers. Look carefully at his profile. Think of extra questions Patsy could ask.

What kind of …?

Make notes here
_____
_____
_____
_____

Use extra information about Ross. He chatted to Patsy at the City Hall. What did he tell her?

I'm interested in …   I like …

Make notes here
_____
_____
_____
_____

Remember to set out the interview like a play.

The names of the interviewer and the interviewee are on the left. The words they say come after their names. Remember the interview between Patsy and Laura:

Patsy: Why did you want to do this project?
Laura: I thought it sounded interesting.

Unit 1 Planning sheet for writing an interview

Listening and speaking

1 Complete the dialogue. Use the verbs and expressions from the boxes.

| like | think | live | have got | go | be interested |

| It sounds … | Lucky you! | me, too! | Hmm | at all |

Laura: Where do you live, Holly?
Holly: I _____ in a flat near the station.
Laura: _____ you _____ any brothers or sisters?
Holly: Yes, I _____ a brother and two sisters.
Laura: _____! I've only got one brother. Which school _____ you _____ to?
Holly: I _____ to Central High School. I _____ it's a great school. We _____ a swimming pool, a library and a theatre.
Laura: _____ fantastic! _____ you _____ in swimming?
Holly: No, I don't like swimming _____. I _____ to the library every week, though. I _____ reading books.
Laura: What sort of books _____ you _____?
Holly: _____ … I _____ mystery stories best.
Laura: Oh, _____!

Individual speaking

1 Think about your family. Who lives in your home?

| mum | dad | brother | sister | aunt | uncle | cousin | grandma | grandpa | anyone else? |

2 Make notes about your family. Use the questions below or use your own ideas.

- Who is in your family? Write one name on the first line in each box.
- Who goes to work? What jobs do they do? Write the jobs under the names.
- Who goes to school? Write the name of the school under the names.
- What are the people in your family interested in? Add notes to the boxes.
- What things do they like? Add notes to the boxes.

3 Write sentences about the people in your family. Use your notes in the boxes.

4 Talk to the class for one minute. Tell them about your family.

Check-out 1

Reading

1   You read a magazine article.

   a   What was the title of the article? _____

   b   What was the full name of the project? _____

2   There was an interview between two people.

   a   Who were they? _____   _____

   b   Who was the interviewee? _____   c   Who was the interviewer? _____

Vocabulary

1   You learned 20 words about working on a group project. Look at page 122 in this book.

   Do you know what all these words mean? Check any that you are not sure of in your dictionary.

2   Is a suffix added to the end of the word or the beginning of a word? _____

3   Make these verbs into nouns. Write the nouns. Use the suffixes -tion or -ment. Check
   Student's Book page 11 if you are not sure and learn the words.

   a   present _____   b   excite _____   c   argue _____   d   imagine _____

4   Complete these words with sh or ss. If you are not sure, check in your dictionary.

   a   se____ion   b   fa____ion   c   impre____ion   d   mi____ion   e   cu____ion

Grammar

1   Maisie is talking about her family. Complete the paragraph. Use be, work, live, think, like.

   I _____ with my family in the centre of the city. My dad _____ an engineer.
   Usually, he _____ in the city but right now, he _____ in France so he _____
   not _____ at home. He _____ his job is interesting but I _____ not interested
   in engineering. I _____ puzzles and quizzes but we both _____ designing things.

Writing

1   Complete these features of an interview.

   An interview is set out like a _____. The names of the speakers are on the _____.
   The words they say are on the _____. The interviewer _____ the questions.
   The interviewee _____ the questions.

2   Have you made a neat copy of your interview? ☐   Is it in your folder? ☐

Listening and speaking

1   Have you listened again to Jack and Ross? ☐

2   Did your friend ask you about your home and family, and things you like and dislike? ☐

3   Did you ask your friend? ☐

4   Have you talked for one minute about your family? ☐

Check-out 1 complete ☐

2 City life

Reading comprehension

1 Read *The man at the fountain* again.

2 Complete the sentences.
1. The square was __bustling__ on this hot afternoon.
2. Buses with __dusty__ windows were cruising around the square.
3. Blue-grey __fumes__ rose into the air.
4. He was almost hidden by a group of tourists with __clicking__ cameras.
5. It was made from white marble that __glistened__ like Arctic ice.
6. He took several photos of the __square__.
7. It had six white __columns__ at the front.
8. It used to belong to a __duke__.
9. Philippe __frowned__ and stared harder at the man.
10. Startled __pigeons__ took off in a cloud of grey.

3 Answer these questions. Use short answers.
1. How did Philippe know that the man was a thief? <u>Because his picture was in the newspapers.</u>
2. What things were being sold in the square? __newspapers, cold drinks, snacks and ice-cream stall.__
3. Where did the buses stop? __under a tree.__
4. Why was the thief difficult to recognise? __he was in disguise__
5. Which people were looking for the man? __The police__
6. Which people were almost hiding the thief? __group of tourists__
7. What were in the four corners of the fountain? __huge, leaping fish__
8. Who called out to Philippe? __his cousin__
9. Who used to own the elegant building? __It used to belong a duke.__
10. Why could Philippe not see the thief after the tourists left? __because the ice-cream seller moved his cart__

4 Answer these questions. Check your answer with the text. If the text does not tell you the answer, write *I can't tell*.
1. Who was Philippe waiting for? __his cousin.__
2. What was his cousin doing? __selling newspapers__
3. Where were they going to go together? __a match__
4. Did they go to the match? __No.__
5. Did Philippe plan to follow the thief? __Yes__
6. Did Philippe follow the thief? __Yes__

12 Unit 2 Reading comprehension: cloze; inferential questions

Vocabulary

1 Read the words in the box.

strut	entrance	movement	hum	hiss	shade
drift	spurt	gape	mingle	snack	click
pigeon	cascade	scent	glisten	chariot	coo	cruise

They were used as verbs or nouns in the text. Underline the verbs.
List all the words under the correct word class.
First, work without looking in the text or your dictionary. Next, use the text to help you.
Finally, check in your dictionary if you need to.

verbs (11) _spurt_ _strut_ _coo_ _drift_ _hum_ _hiss_
click _glisten_ _cruise_ _____ _____

nouns (8) _pigeon_ _snack_ _shade_ _entrance_ _movement_ _chariot_
cascade _scent_

2 Read these verbs.

| strut | cruise | drift | spurt | mingle | dart |

Do the verbs express different kinds of sound, movement or appearance? _____

3 Write the verbs in Exercise 2 next to the correct definition.

1 to travel smoothly and easily _____
2 to move quickly and suddenly _____
3 to go slowly without a clear direction _____
4 to walk around among other people _____
5 to flow out very fast _____
6 to walk in a very proud way, feeling important _____

4 Find these verbs from the verb list in Exercise 1.

1 the verb that means: to shine and appear as if a little bit wet _____
2 four verbs that express sounds _____ _____ _____ _____

5 Choose the correct noun from Exercise 1 to complete these sentences.

1 I always have a small _____ when I get home from school.
2 Sit in the _____ so you don't get burned by the sun.
3 You can see lots of _____ in the squares in London.
4 In the past, people used to race with horses and _____.
5 This rose is pretty but it doesn't have any _____.
6 A _____ of water fell from the mountain into the river.

6 Find adjectives in the text that mean the same or nearly the same as these words.

1 busy _____   2 wide open _____   3 beautiful _____
4 wide _____   5 surprised _____   6 wonderful _____

Unit 2 Vocabulary: descriptive verbs and nouns

Working with words

1 **Rewrite each pair of sentences as one sentence. Use the present participle as an adjective.**

1 The baby was crying. He woke everyone. *The crying baby woke everyone.*
2 The water was falling. It splashed into the pool. _____
3 Ben could hear the boys. The boys were laughing. _____
4 Children were running. They hurried to the school. _____
5 Can you hear the lions? The lions are roaring. _____

Read these phrases. They should be in your answers. Check.

| The crying baby | The falling water | the laughing boys | Running children | the roaring lions |

2 **Rewrite the sentences as one sentence using the present participle as an adjective.**

Ben was woken by the lightning. The lightning was flashing.

Ben was woken by the flashing lightning.

1 The phone was ringing. It was answered by the man.
_____

2 Harry was frightened of the snake. The snake was hissing.
_____

3 The man was drowning. He was saved by the rescue team.
_____

4 Andy tried to catch the glass. The glass was falling.
_____

3 **Add the prefix *un-*, *dis-* or *re-* to these words to make new words.**

1 _dis_ agree   2 _re_ do   3 _dis_ believe
4 _re_ write   5 _re_ tie   6 _un_ fair

Check the rules in your Student's Book if you need to.

4 **abc Spelling: make these verbs into nouns by adding -er.**

1 cut — *cutter*
2 travel — *traveller*
3 wander — *wanderer* ✓

5 **abc Write the past tense of these verbs.**

1 refer — *referred*
2 discover — *discovered*
3 cancel — *cancelled*
4 stop — *stopped*
5 cook — *cooked* ✓

6 **abc Make these adjectives into adverbs.**

1 careful — *carefully*
2 slow — *slowly*
3 final — *finally*
4 quick — *quickly*
5 general — *generally* ✓

7 **abc Write the present continuous of these verbs.**

1 hit   2 quarrel   3 drop   4 gallop   5 wonder

_____ _____ _____ _____ _____

Unit 2 Working with words: present participle as adjective; prefixes; Spelling: doubling before suffixing

Grammar

1 Complete the sentences with the words in the box. Use the past simple.

| slide | be | rise | take | know | want | sell | stand | go |

1 Philippe _____ that the man _____ a thief.
2 The man _____ among the tourists.
3 He _____ not _____ anyone to recognise him.
4 Nobody _____ any notice of him.
5 The man suddenly _____ a slim camera from his pocket.
6 Every day Philippe's cousin _____ newspapers in the square.
7 Fumes from the buses _____ into the air.
8 Philippe _____ not _____ to the football match that afternoon.

2 Complete the sentences with the words in the box. Use the past continuous.

| fly | glisten | look | bustle | sell | click | wear | enjoy |

1 The square _____ with visitors.
2 _____ they _____ the warm weather?
3 Their cameras _____ busily.
4 What _____ Philippe's cousin _____?
5 The thief _____ a disguise.
6 The police _____ everywhere for this man.
7 A flag _____ above the entrance to the bank.
8 The marble fountain _____ in the sunlight.

3 Complete the sentences with the verbs in brackets.
Use the past simple and the past continuous.

1 When Philippe _____ the square, he _____ a crowd of tourists.
   (enter, see)
2 While Philippe _____ the tourists, he _____ the thief. (watch, notice)
3 The thief _____ with the tourists when Philippe _____ him.
   (mingle, spot)
4 While he _____ the fountain, he suddenly _____ his camera at the bank.
   (photograph, point)
5 Philippe _____ that the man _____ suspiciously. (think, behave)
6 When the thief suddenly _____ away, Philippe _____ to follow him.
   (run, decide)
7 Perhaps the man _____ that Philippe _____ him. (know, watch)
8 The thief _____ to escape from the boy who _____ him. (try, follow)

Unit 2 Grammar: past simple; past continuous; *while* and *when*

Grammar in use

1 Complete the sentences with the words in the boxes.

| used to | | make | ride | have | be | sell | cross |

1 Years ago the castle _used to be_ a prison.
2 An old wooden bridge _used to cross_ the river but now it's gone.
3 That shop _used to sell_ books but now it's a sports shop.
4 When he was younger, my grandfather _used to ride_ a motorbike.
5 My grandmother _used to make_ her own clothes.
6 When we were younger, we _used to have_ more free time.

2 Write questions for the answers.

1 *Did the town use to be much smaller?* Yes, the town used to be much smaller.
2 _Did there use to be a park?_ Yes, there used to be a park.
3 Where _did the castle use to be?_ The castle used to stand outside the town.
4 How often _did the children use to visit their grandparents?_ The children used to visit their grandparents once a month.
5 _Did they use to live on a farm?_ No, they didn't use to live on a farm.
6 What _did you use to play when you were young?_ When we were little, we used to play with dolls and trains.

3 Disagree! Make the sentences negative.

1 The children used to walk to school. **No, they didn't use to walk to school.**
2 We used to go to the cinema. _No, we didn't use to go to the cinema._
3 That man used to be an actor. _No, that man didn't use to be an actor._
4 Alice used to play the violin. _No, Alice didn't use to play the violin._
5 Mr Jones used to live in Italy. _No, Mr Jones didn't use to live in Italy._
6 The babies used to cry a lot. _No, the babies didn't use to cry a lot._

4 Complete the sentences with the words in the boxes.

| make | take | | notice | a photo | escape | a holiday | mistakes |

1 The boy was shouting angrily but nobody _takes_ any _notice_ of him.
2 Be careful not to _make_ any _mistakes_ in your test.
3 Harry's exhausted. He needs to _take a holiday_.
4 Let's _take a photo_ of the marble fountain.
5 The prisoner jumped over the wall and _make_ his _escape_.

Individual writing: descriptive writing

You have read a **description** of the square on a hot afternoon. You have written a **description** of the square at night. Now write a **description** of the square in the rain.

Read Student's Book page 24 again. It tells you how to write a **description**.

Make notes:

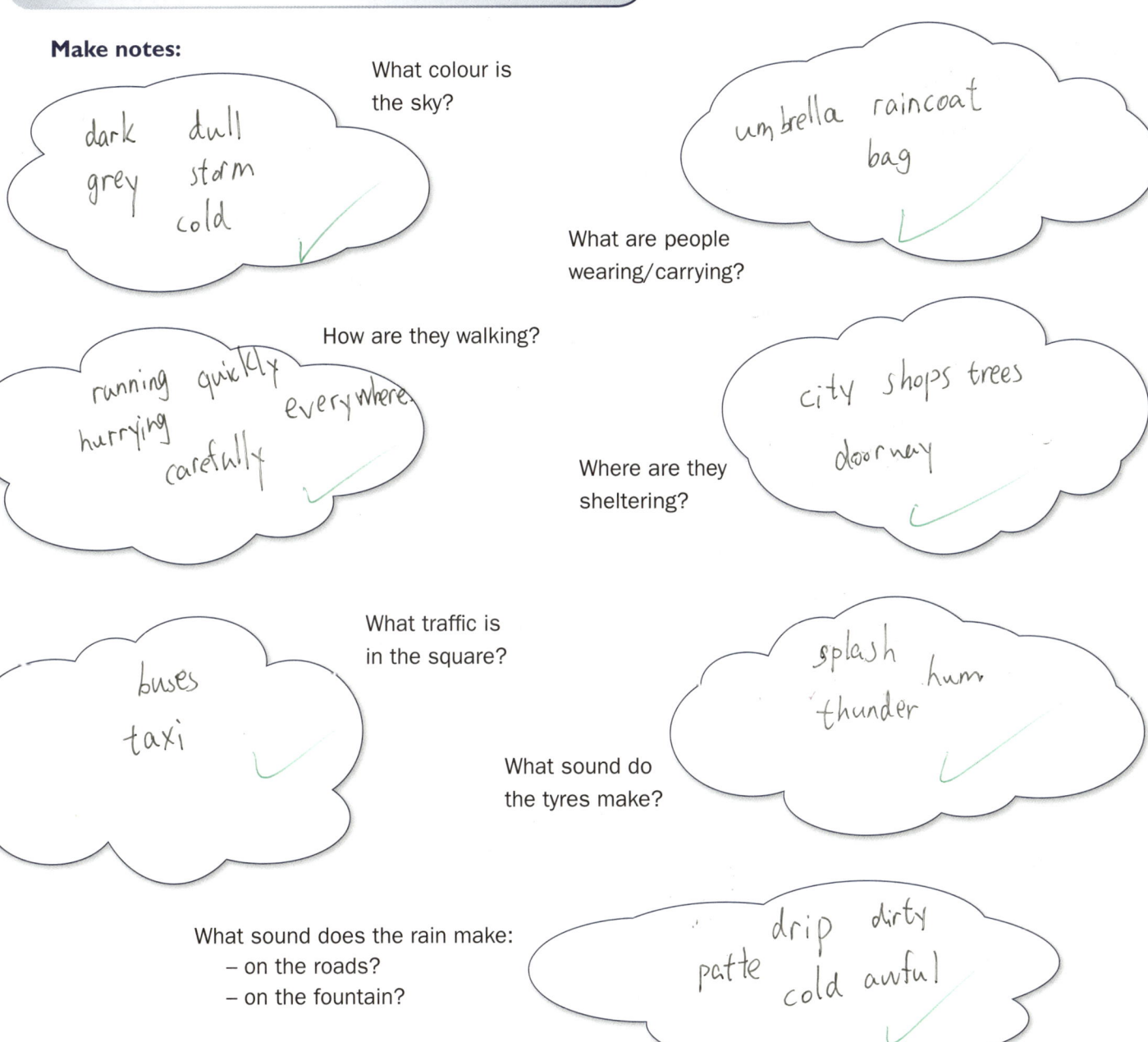

What colour is the sky? — dark, dull, grey, storm, cold ✓

What are people wearing/carrying? — umbrella, raincoat, bag ✓

How are they walking? — running, quickly, hurrying, carefully, everywhere ✓

Where are they sheltering? — city, shops, trees, doorway ✓

What traffic is in the square? — buses, taxi ✓

What sound do the tyres make? — splash, hum, thunder ✓

What sound does the rain make:
 – on the roads?
 – on the fountain?
— patter, drip, dirty, cold, awful ✓

Here are some useful words you could use:

Adjectives	awful	gloomy	grey	cloudy
	cold	dull	dirty	dry
Adverbs	carefully	everywhere	quickly	
Nouns	city	cloud	doorway	umbrella
	shop	lorry	storm	thunder
Verbs	rumble	splash	drip	hiss
	patter	screech		

Now write your description of the square.

Unit 2 Planning sheet for describing settings | 7

Listening and speaking

1 Complete the dialogue. Use the words and expressions from the boxes.

was	were	~~use~~	used	went	liked	~~hate~~
wear	~~like~~	ugly	lovely	horrible	favourite	

Me too!	Poor you!	Lucky you!
Really?	How about you?	

Laura: Which primary school did you __use__ to go to?
Holly: Green Oak School. __How about you__?
Laura: I __went__ to Mill Road School.
Holly: What __were__ your teachers __like__?
Laura: They were __lovely__. My __favourite__ was Miss Bun. She __used__ to teach us science.
Holly: Did you have to __wear__ a uniform?
Laura: Yes, I __like__ my uniform.
Holly: __Lucky you__! Mine was __horrible__.
Laura: __Really__? Why?
Holly: It was uncomfortable and __ugly__.
Laura: __Poor you__! What colour __was__ it?
Holly: Black and orange. I __hate__ the colour orange.
Laura: __Me too__!

Individual speaking

1 You are going to interview an older member of your family about their childhood. Who will you choose? Your grandma or grandpa? An aunt or an uncle? Someone else? Write at least six questions. Use the words and phrases in the box to help you.

Where – live?	house or apartment?	brothers and sisters?
parents' jobs?	school?	free time?	games?

For example:
Where did you use to live when you were young?

My questions for __my mom__

Do you need to wear school uniform?
Do you like your school?

2 Ask your questions and make notes.

3 Write sentences about your family member's childhood. Use your notes.

4 Talk about your family member's childhood for one minute.

Unit 2 Listening and speaking: completing a dialogue; Individual speaking: an older family member's childhood

Check-out 2

Reading

1 You read a descriptive story. a What place in the city was the setting? _____

   b What structure was described in detail in the story? _____

2 The story described things that Philippe could see, hear and smell. Write the correct sense after each phrase.

   a the scent of roses _____ b tinkling water _____ c glistened like Arctic ice _____

Vocabulary

1 You learned words describing the city square. Look at page 122 in this book.
   Do you know what all these words mean? Check any that you are not sure of in your dictionary.

2 Read this sentence: The running man quickly disappeared from sight.

   a What is the main verb? _____ b Which is the present participle? _____

   c What word class is the present participle in this sentence? _____

3 Look at this word: **unhelpful**. Write: the root word _____ the suffix _____ the prefix _____

4 Write the past tense of these verbs.

   a travel _____ b refer _____ c discover _____ d quarrel _____

Grammar

1 Complete these sentences. Choose the past simple or the past continuous.

   While the tourists _____ (take) photos of the statues, a police car _____ (arrive) in the square. The policeman _____ (walk) towards the fountain, when someone suddenly _____ (shout) "Stop, thief!"

2 Complete this sentence with the correct form of used to.

   Jack: I never _____ go to school by car. Did you _____ go by car?

   Ross: No, I _____ go by car, either. I _____ go to school by bus.

3 Complete with make or take. _____ notice of the rules so you don't _____ mistakes.

Writing

1 Complete these features of a descriptive story.

   It is written in the _____ tense. The writer often uses _____ to tell the reader more about the nouns. The writer describes what you can see. Often, the writer also describes what you can _____ and _____.

2 Have you made a neat copy of your description of the square in the rain? ☐ Is it in your folder? ☐

Listening and speaking

1 Have you listened again to Jack and Ross? ☐

2 Did you and your friend talk about your old primary schools? ☐

3 Have you told the class about a family member's childhood? ☐

Check-out 2 complete ☐

Revision 1 (Units 1 and 2)

1 Complete the sentences with the verbs in brackets. Use the present simple, present continuous, past simple or past continuous.

1 While Professor Brown _____ to the volunteers, some reporters from the local newspaper _____. (speak, arrive)

2 When Professor Brown _____ speaking, the students _____ to pick up leaflets about the project. (finish, rush)

3 Holly Carter _____ to Central High School but today she _____ not _____ in the classroom. She _____ to Professor Brown at City Hall. (go, sit, listen)

4 What's your opinion of the *Portrait* project? I _____ it _____ excellent. (think, sound)

5 Laura _____ surfing the internet. Ross and Jack _____ doing sports. (like, prefer)

6 Yesterday afternoon Philippe _____ by his cousin's newspaper stall when he _____ the thief. (stand, see)

7 At first the man _____ not _____ that Philippe _____ him. (notice, watch)

8 The man _____ away when he _____ Philippe's eyes on him. (run, feel)

2 Change the sentences. Use *used to*.

1 Years ago no tourists visited the town.
_____

2 The magnificent building belonged to a duke.
_____

3 As a child Philippe often came to the square with his father.
_____

3 Write questions for the answers.

1 Who _____ Patsy is interviewing the professor.
2 Where _____ He teaches at the university.
3 What _____ The boys enjoy swimming.
4 Who _____ He spoke to his cousin.
5 _____ Yes, the man ran away.
6 _____ Yes, he was wearing a disguise.
7 Where _____ Some people were sitting in the shade.

4 Find words which mean the same. Use the words in the box.

| broad | find out | create | discuss | entrance | scent | bustling | portrait | snack |

1 picture n _____
2 a pleasant smell n _____
3 make v _____
4 small meal n _____
5 discover v _____
6 the way in n _____
7 talk about v _____
8 wide adj _____
9 busy adj _____

5 Complete the sentences with words from the box.

| popular | run | spot | movement | enthusiastic | disguise |

1 All the students are _____ about this interesting project.
2 A professor from the university is going to _____ the project.
3 We did not recognise the man because he was in _____.
4 Football is the most _____ sport in our school.
5 The crowd stood still. There was no _____ at all.
6 I managed to _____ a face I knew in the crowd.

6 Make nouns from these verbs by adding the suffix -tion or -ment.

1 invite _____
2 argue _____
3 produce _____
4 equip _____
5 imagine _____
6 construct _____

7 Complete the sentences with make, do or take. Make sure you use the correct form of the verb.

1 You must _____ a decision about your future career.
2 John _____ his homework as soon as he got home.
3 I hope I _____ not _____ any mistakes in the test tomorrow!
4 Don't _____ any notice of what other students are doing in the exam.
5 Don't worry about your new school. You _____ soon _____ friends.
6 Stand still! I want _____ a photo of you.
7 The lion _____ its escape when the cage door was left open.
8 You look very tired. You need _____ a holiday.

Revision 1 (Units 1 and 2)

3 Life at the edge

Reading comprehension

1 Read *Endangered animals in the north* again.

2 Write the statements under the correct animal.

~~Its feet are partly webbed.~~   ~~Its back feet are fully webbed.~~   ~~It dives for its food.~~   ~~It has powerful jaws.~~
~~It waits for its food to come to the surface.~~   ~~It uses small stones as tools.~~   ~~It does not make a den.~~
~~The cubs are born in a den.~~   ~~It often sleeps in a group.~~   ~~Its fur is thick and white.~~

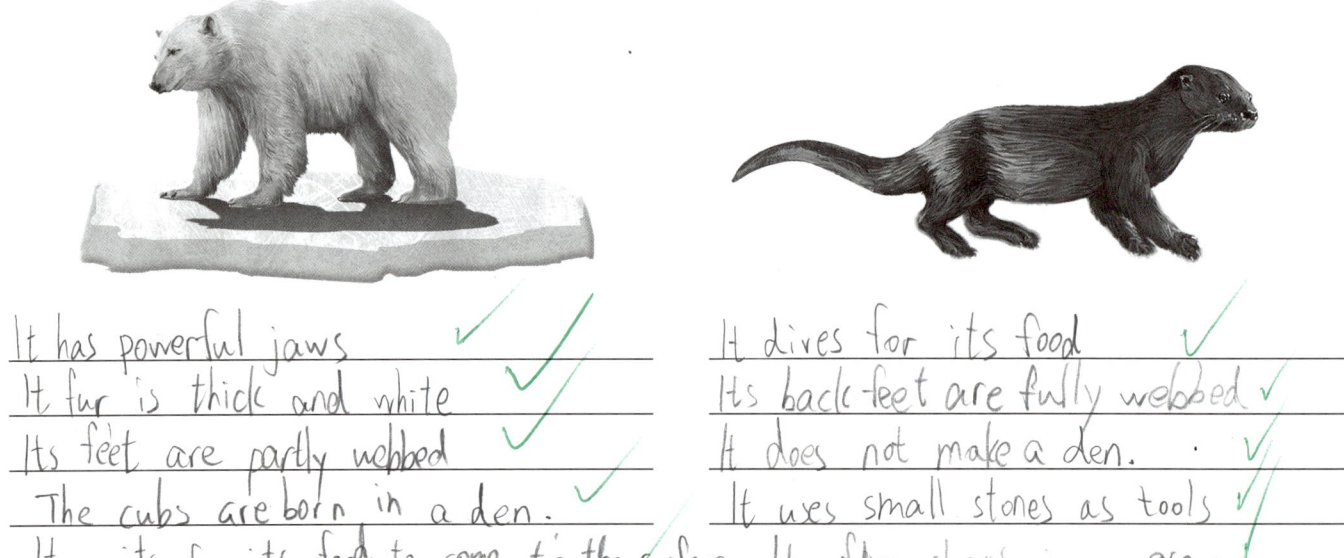

It has powerful jaws ✓
It fur is thick and white ✓
Its feet are partly webbed ✓
The cubs are born in a den. ✓
It waits for its food to come to the surface

It dives for its food ✓
Its back feet are fully webbed ✓
It does not make a den. ✓
It uses small stones as tools ✓
It often sleeps in a group

3 Write the phrases about the polar bear next to the correct word.

Habitat   Sea ice
Appearance   white fur
Diet   seal meat ✓
Reproduction   cubs born in den ✓
Threats   climate change

~~white fur~~
~~seal meat~~
~~sea ice~~
~~climate change~~
~~cubs born in den~~

4 Write the notes about the sea otter next to the correct heading. Try to do this without looking at the text.

~~pups born at sea~~   ~~rocky coasts of the North Pacific~~   ~~thick, waterproof fur~~
~~stays 1 km from the shore~~   ~~searches under boulders~~   ~~new oil fields~~
~~snails, crabs, shellfish~~   ~~oil spills~~   ~~1m–1.5m long~~   ~~bob safely on the surface~~

Habitat   • rocky coasts of the North Pacific. • stays 1 km from the shore ✓
Appearance   • thick, waterproof fur   • 1m–1.5m long
Diet   • snails, crabs, shellfish.   • bob safely on the surface
Reproduction   • pups born at sea.   • searches under boulders
Threats   • oil spills. ✓   • new oil fields

22 Unit 3 Reading comprehension: categorising statements and notes

Vocabulary

1 Write the correct words under the pictures. Use your dictionary to check.

| tanker | raft | seal | oil spill | shore | whiskers |

1 _shore_ 2 _oil spill_ 3 _wiskers_ 4 _raft_ 5 _tanker_ 6 _seal_

2 Write the words next to the correct definition.

| ban | seize | extinct | threaten | insulate | patiently |

1 to grab hold of strongly _seize_
2 died out _extinct_
3 to keep heat in and cold out _insulate_
4 to stop _ban_
5 in an unhurried way without giving up _patiently_
6 to put in danger _threaten_

3 Find the opposite word from the text.

1 male _____ 2 partly _____ 3 freeze _____ 4 guaranteed _____

4 Complete the statements. Find the words in the text.

1 The young of a bear is called a _cub_.
2 The young of a sea otter is called a _pup_.
3 An animal with hair or fur that is born from its mother's body is a _____.
4 The home where a bear lives is called a _____.
5 The white bears in the Arctic are called _____ bears.

5 Complete the sentences. Use the words in the box. Make any necessary changes.

| chest | harmful | prey | snowdrift | bob | newborn |

1 After the blizzard, the explorers got stuck in a deep _snowdrift_.
2 The _newborn_ baby was wrapped in a warm blanket.
3 In the bay, small fishing boats were _bobbing_ up and down on the waves.
4 Too many sweets can be _harmful_ to your teeth.
5 Some birds have brightly coloured feathers on their _chest_.
6 Lions leap on their _prey_ and pull them down to the ground.

Unit 3 Vocabulary; definitions; antonyms; cloze

Working with words

1 **Rewrite these nouns to make adjectives ending -al. Complete the sentences.**

a industry   b fact   c music   d coast   e electric   f nature

industrial   _factual_   _musical_   _coastal_   _electrical_   _natural_

1 Max is very _musical_ and he is learning the trumpet.
2 My cousin is studying _electrical_ engineering at college.
3 Does pollution only come from _industrial_ areas?
4 Dolphins leap high out of the water and this is _natural_ behaviour.
5 The _coastal_ waters are full of fish and other sea creatures.
6 I prefer _factual_ books as I find them more interesting than stories.

Think about the spelling!

2 **Write three sentences of your own. Use the words in the box.**

| normal | several | final |

_____
_____
_____

3 **Rewrite these nouns to make adjectives ending -y. Complete the sentences.**

a silk   b thirst   c scare   d fun   e hunger   f stone

silky   _thirsty_   _scary_   _funny_   _hungry_   _stony_

1 The boys were _hungry_ so they made a pizza.
2 We saw a really _scary_ film which I didn't like at all.
3 The cat's fur felt soft and _silky_ under my fingers.
4 If you are _thirsty_ you can get a drink from the fridge.
5 We followed the guide along a _stony_ path.
6 When the bucket fell on my head, everyone thought it was really _funny_

Mind your spelling!

4 **Spelling: look at the pictures. Complete the sentences. Use words with *ei* or *ie*.**

1 The _____ was full of _____ when he _read_ the letter.

2 That _____ has stolen Dad's _____! _____ him!

3 The _____ of my best _____ is 1.5 metres. Her _____ is 50kg.

24 Unit 3 Working with words: adjectives ending with suffixes -al, -y; Spelling: *ei / ie*

Grammar

1 Complete the sentences with *will* and a verb from the box.

~~hunt~~   ~~threaten~~   ~~become~~   ~~survive~~   ~~live~~   ~~melt~~

1. __Will__ polar bears __survive__ if their habitat disappears?
2. The bears __will live__ in safety in Russia's new Arctic Park.
3. People __will__ not __hunt__ animals in the Arctic Park.
4. Experts believe that next year the snow __melt__ earlier.
5. Sea otters __will become__ extinct if they are not protected.
6. An oil spill in this area __will threaten__ the sea otters' habitat.

2 Complete the sentences with the correct form of *going to* and a verb from the box.

~~do~~
~~drive~~
find
~~observe~~
~~spend~~
learn

1. A team of experts __are going to observe__ the behaviour of otters.
2. They __are going to spend__ a month at Cape Erimo.
3. They __are going to drive__ to the coast in two 4x4s.
4. We __are going to learn__ about animals in danger.
5. I __am going to do__ a project on polar bears.
6. My friend __is going to find__ photos on the internet.

3 Write questions for the answers.

1. What __are they going to film?__
   They are going to film the wildlife in the area.
2. How __will they travel?__
   They'll travel in two old 4x4s.
3. __Are they going to count the otters?__
   Yes, they're going to count the otters.
4. __Is it going to be very hard work?__
   Yes, it's going to be very hard work.
5. Who __will lead the team?__
   Professor Ball will lead the team.
6. When __do you finish your project.__
   I'll finish my project by the end of next week.

4 Write short answers.

1. Is he going to leave? __Yes, he is.__
2. Are they going to drive? No, __they aren't.__
3. Will the ice melt? No, __it won't.__
4. Are you going to swim? Yes, __I am.__
5. Is it going to snow? No, __it isn't.__
6. Will the bears survive? No, __they won't.__
7. Will they see otters? Yes, __they will.__
8. Are you going to leave? No, __I'm not.__

Grammar in use

1 Look at the computer. What are the teenagers doing for *The portrait project* and when?

> **The portrait project**
> **Monday:** Laura, Ross and Jack – sports centre – report on basketball team.
> **Friday:** Holly and Ross – visit Professor Bolt at his house. Holly: interview him. Ross: draw a portrait.
> **Next week:** Everyone to the shopping centre. Laura – take photos. Interview shoppers. Record interviews.

Answer the questions.

1 Where are Laura, Ross and Jack going on Monday? _They are going to the sports centre_
2 What are they doing there? _they are reporting on basketball team._
3 When are Holly and Ross visiting Professor Bolt? _They're visiting on Friday._
4 Who is interviewing him? _____
5 What is Ross doing? _____
6 Who is going to the shopping centre? _____
7 What is Laura doing? _____
8 Are they writing down their interviews? _____

2 Write about your plans.

1 What are you doing tomorrow? _____
2 What are you doing at the weekend? _____
3 What are you doing next month? _____
4 Are you doing anything exciting this year? _____
5 What is your family doing this week? Write about two members of your family.

_____
_____

3 Complete the sentences with *catch* and the words in the box.

| eye | fire | a cold | the bus | a glimpse |

1 You must hurry if you want to _____ _____.
2 In the music shop a silver electric guitar _____ Sam's _____.
3 Why is Sally sniffing? _____ she _____ _____?
4 As we drove through the forest, we _____ _____ of the sea between the trees.
5 A flash of lightning hit the roof and the house _____ _____.

26 Unit 3 Grammar in use: present continuous for future events; Grammar extra: phrasal verbs with *catch*

Individual writing: writing a report from notes

You have looked at the stages of **research** and writing **notes** about polar bears and sea otters. Now you are going to read these **notes** and write a **report** about the giant panda.

Read Student's Book page 34 again. It tells you about how to write a **report**.

Read these notes about the giant panda.

> giant panda - once in central / west / south China
> now only central China
> 2,000 = wild / 180 in captivity
> 75cms tall / males: 113kg / females: 100kg
> body is mainly white - black ears, black around the eyes, nose, shoulders and legs
> lives about 30 years in zoos
> lives alone
> gives birth to single cub - stays with mother for 18 months
> eats bamboo / small animals / vegetation
> does not hibernate
> small numbers: bamboo cut down / hunted

Use these notes to write a report about the giant panda.

Giant panda

The giant panda lives in the central china. It has thick, white and black fur, they are heavy, the males are 113 kg and the females are 100kg. Their body is mainly white - black ears, black around the eyes, nose, shoulders and legs. They gives birth to single cub - stays with mother for 18 months, and they eat bamboos, small animals and vegtation, it does not hibernate. They are smaller numbers of panda because people are cutting down the bamboos.

well done Jerry!

If you need more space, use another piece of paper.

Listening and speaking

1 Complete the dialogue. Use the verbs and expressions from the boxes.

take	meet	play	do	get	Lucky you!	So	Well	What else
come	go	spend	buy	swim	How about you?	You, too		

Holly: _____ ... what _____ you _____ this weekend, Jack?
Jack: _____, on Sunday I _____ the afternoon at the sports centre.
Holly: Really? _____ you _____ basketball?
Jack: No, I'm not. I _____ with some friends.
Holly: That sounds fun. _____ are you doing?
Jack: Laura and I _____ to London.
Holly: Wow! _____! How _____ you _____ there?
Jack: We're going by train. Mum _____ us. I can't wait. _____? What are you doing?
Holly: Well, on Saturday morning I _____ some new shoes and in the afternoon I _____ my cousin at the station. She _____ to stay for the weekend.
Jack: Well, have a good time.
Holly: Thanks. _____.

Individual speaking

Think about something which you are going to do in the future. Perhaps you are going on a trip or having a holiday. Perhaps you are going shopping or visiting someone. What are your plans?

2 Read the questions and make notes.

Where are you going? _____ When? _____
Why? _____
How are you travelling? _____
Who are you going with? _____
What are you doing when you get there? _____
_____
_____
_____
_____
_____
How long are you staying there? _____
When are you coming back? _____

3 Write sentences about your plans. Use your notes.

4 Talk to the class about your plans.

28 Unit 3 Listening and speaking: completing a dialogue; Individual speaking: future plans

Check-out 3

Reading

1. You read information about two animals. a What were they? ~~polar bear~~ ~~sea otter~~
   b What part of the world do they live in? ~~Arctic~~

2. The information was divided into five _____ with sub-headings.
   They covered five aspects of the animals' lives. What were they?
   h~~abitat~~, a~~ppearace~~, d~~iet~~, r~~eproduction~~, ~~threats~~.

Vocabulary

1. You learned 20 words about animals and habitat. Look at page 122 in this book.
   Do you know what all these words mean? Check any that you are not sure of in your dictionary.

2. Make these nouns into adjectives using the suffix -al or -y. Check your spelling.
   a industry ~~al~~   b hand ~~y~~   c fact ~~al~~   d star ~~ry~~   e electric ~~al~~

3. Complete these words with ei or ie.
   a rec__ __ve   b h~~ei~~ght   c gr__ __f   d th__ __f   e s__ __ze

Grammar

1. Complete the sentences with will or going to.
   a Listen to the thunder! There _____ be a big storm.
   b The next train to Hampton _____ leave from platform 2.

2. Circle the correct tense and complete the sentence.
   You can use the present simple / present continuous / present perfect for future meaning.
   Holly _____ (visit) her cousins at the weekend.

3. Tick the things you can catch.   a cold ___   a journey ___   a train ___   a glimpse ___   a view ___

Writing

1. Underline the correct words in italics.
   When you write notes you have to / should not write in complete sentences.
   When you write a first draft you must / need not write in complete sentences.
   A report / paragraph / draft is a group of sentences about one subject.

2. Have you made a neat copy of your information about the panda? ☐   Is it in your folder? ☐

Listening and speaking

1. Have you listened again to Laura and Ross? ☐
2. Did your friend tell you about his/her plans for this weekend? ☐
3. Did you tell your friend about your plans for this weekend? ☐
4. Have you talked for one minute about something you are going to do in the future? ☐

Check-out 3 complete ☐

4 Advertisements

Reading comprehension

1 Read the advert for the *Adventure Sports Centre* again.

2 Label the activities.

bungee jump   aerial runway   indoor sky-diving   suspended bridge   vertical slide   climbing wall

1 Indoor skydiving
2 Climbing wall
3 aerial runway
4 vertical slide
5 bungee jump
6 suspended bridge

3 Answer the questions about the Centre. Use short answers.
1. How much do members get off entry to the centre on any day? _10%_
2. What do they get on selected weekends? _half price_
3. When is the centre open to members only? _evening sessions_
4. Where can you go sky-diving at the centre? _Indoors_
5. What other membership comes with membership of the Adventure Sports Centre? _Sports Park Complex_
6. What two items do members get free? _T-shirt and bag_
7. How many free training sessions can members have every year? _one_
8. How many people must be in a member's group booking to get a 15% reduction? _10% or more_
9. Which main road is the Sports Park Complex on? _North Avenue_
10. How far is the complex from the motorway? _1km_

4 Answer the questions. Use complete sentences.
1. What surprised the boy who climbed the wall?
The boy thought he couldn't climb so high but he could.
2. What does the girl who has never been sky-diving want to do?
She wants to do Indoor Skydiving.
3. How long has the boy who is a member been a member?
He has been a member for a year.
4. Did the girl who went down the vertical slide enjoy it? Which words tell you?
Yes, because she said unbelievable, Unforgettable and Unmissable.

Vocabulary

1 Write the words next to the correct definition.

| reduce | contact | select | provide | suspend |

1 to choose _____
2 to make less _____
3 to speak or write to someone _____
4 to hang _____
5 to give _____

2 Complete the sentences with the verbs in Exercise 1. Make any necessary changes.

1 _____ the CD that you want then pay for it at the check-out.
2 Coloured lights were _____ between the trees in the park.
3 We had to _____ my uncle quickly when Grandpa was ill.
4 You can _____ the number of mistakes in your work if you read it through.
5 The teacher _____ paper for the children to draw on.

3 Write the letter of the correct definition next to each phrase.

1 bird's eye view ____   a what a bird sees from a height   b a close look at a bird's eye
2 10% off ____   a 10% fewer   b 10% less
3 qualified trainers ____   a people who have passed tests for teaching people how to do things   b a good pair of shoes for sports
4 automatic membership ____   a members can bring cars   b becoming a member happens anyway
5 members-only session ____   a a time just for members   b a time for just one member

4 Write the words next to the correct definition.

| swoop | challenge | qualify | motorway | skill |

1 to compete against _____
2 ability to do something well _____
3 to dive smoothly through the air _____
4 to pass the necessary tests or exams _____
5 a very wide road taking fast traffic long distances _____

5 Write the verbs that are the root words for these nouns.

1 qualification _____   2 reduction _____   3 selection _____

Working with words

1 Rewrite the adjectives to make nouns.

1 different _____
2 silent _____
3 excellent _____
4 patient _____
5 obedient _____
6 confident _____
7 evident _____

2 Complete the sentences with the correct adjective or noun from Exercise 1.

1 There wasn't a single sound in the cave and the _____ was a little bit scary.
2 Ben has a lot of _____ and I'm sure he'll get an _____ mark in the exam.
3 The police searched for _____ of the crime.
4 What's the main _____ between a shark and a dolphin?
5 We must wait an hour for the train so please stand still and be _____.
6 The horse's _____ was amazing – it followed every command from the rider.
7 I'm not _____ about my project so I'm going to choose a _____ subject.

3 Write the word class after each word.

1 obey _____
2 obedient _____
3 obediently _____
4 obedience _____

4 Rewrite the adjectives to make nouns.

1 important _____
2 brilliant _____
3 elegant _____
4 defiant _____
5 ignorant _____
6 reliant _____
7 distant _____

5 Complete the sentences with the correct adjective or noun from Exercise 4.

1 The _____ of the city lights could be seen in the _____.
2 The dancer performed with style and _____.
3 It's _____ to learn the school rules so that you don't disobey out of _____.
4 The naughty boy was _____ and would not obey his teacher.
5 If you are completely _____ on the internet, you will have problems when your computer crashes.

6 Write the word class after each word.

1 ignorance _____
2 ignorantly _____
3 ignore _____
4 ignorant _____

7 abc Spelling: complete the words in this paragraph. Write ou or oo.

The gr_____p of w_____nded soldiers t_____k off their b_____ts and put their feet in the c_____l p_____l. Then they t_____k the fastest r_____te to the camp where they c_____ld rest and the cook w_____ld give them bowls of hot s_____p.

---

32 Unit 4 Working with words: words ending -ence and -ance; word classes; Spelling: ou / oo

Grammar

1 Complete the sentences with the verbs in the box. Use the present perfect.

fall   become   be   swim   hear   try   see   drive

1 Miranda John __has__ always __been__ keen on sport.
2 Miranda and Jason __have tried__ many different sports.
3 __Have__ you ever __swam__ in the sea?
4 That rider __has fell__ off his horse many times.   has fallen
5 These Formula 1 drivers __have drove__ on racetracks all over the world.   driven
6 I __have__ never __seen__ a more exciting basketball match.
7 __Have__ you __heard__ the football results on the radio?
8 Kite-surfing __has became__ more popular recently.

2 What has happened? Look at the pictures and write sentences. Use the present perfect.

Oh, no! Where is it?

Look! We can skate!

1 The mountaineers __have climbed to the summit of the mountain.__
2 __She has won the gold medal for the Olinpic.__   Olympics
3 __The boy has broken his leg.__
4 __The woman has lost her watch.__
5 __A bird has built a nest.__
6 __Two people have chopped the trees.__   archaeologist
7 __Two men have skated on the ice.__
8 __The archaeologist has found a statue.__

3 What have you done recently? Write three sentences. Use the present perfect.

1 This month __I have been to the park.__
2 This week __I have studied.__
3 Today __I have been to school.__

Unit 4 Grammar: present perfect (action happening at an indefinite time in the past; past action with present result)   33

Grammar in use

1 Write sentences. Use the present perfect.
1. Luke – play – basketball – several years Luke has played basketball for several years
2. The players – train – hard – a long time The players have trained hard for a long time.
3. People – grow – cotton – this area – the last century People have grown cotton in this area for the last century
4. We – live – our apartment – last summer We have lived in our apartment since last summer.
5. You – wear – those glasses – ages You have worn those glasses for ages
6. Jenny – be – hospital – March Jenny has been in the hospital since March.

2 Write the sentences again. Use the present perfect and *just*.
1. Lucy spoke to her grandmother a short while ago. Lucy has just spoken to her grandmother
2. Someone took my bag a moment ago. Someone has taken my bag
3. The students ate their lunch a few minutes ago. The students have just eaten their lunch
4. John bought some CDs a minute ago. John has just bought some CDs
5. I saw something very strange a moment ago. I have just seen something.
6. We heard the news a few minutes ago. We have just heard the news a few minutes ago

3 Write the sentences correctly.
1. the Has match yet? finished _____
2. team yet. scored Our hasn't _____
3. joined club you the yet? sports Have _____
4. tunnel haven't the yet. We wind tried _____
5. have players yet. not the The won trophy _____
6. you yet? wall been the Have up climbing _____

4 Complete the sentences with one of the phrasal verbs in the box. Be sure to use the correct form of the verb.

| bring up | bring forward | bring out | bring back | bring round |

1. Uncle Ted went on holiday to India and _____ presents for everyone.
2. At first Henry disagreed with us but finally we _____ him _____ to our way of thinking.
3. Mandy's grandmother was _____ on a farm in America.
4. That factory is going to _____ a car that uses solar power.
5. We decided to _____ our holiday _____ from August to July.

Unit 4 Grammar in use: present perfect with *for*, *since*, *just* and *yet*; Grammar extra: phrasal verbs with *bring*

Individual writing: writing to persuade

4

You have read about the Adventure Sports Centre. The advert used words and pictures to **persuade** you to visit. Now, imagine a school team is in a competition with three other schools. You are going to design a handout **advertising** the competition and **persuading** people to come.

Read Student's Book page 44 again. It tells you about **persuasive** writing.

What sports teams do you have in your school?

Choose the sport you are most interested in: _____

Make notes:

- a name for your team _____

- handout heading
  – remember to make it interesting!

- Information
  date: _____
  time: _____
  venue: _____

Use this to plan how your handout will look.
Remember to think about:
colour / illustration / size of letters.

Some useful **persuasive** words:	
amazing	astonishing
brilliant	electrifying
entertaining	excellent
exciting	exhilarating
incredible	magnificent
spectacular	thrilling

Unit 4 Planning sheet for persuasive writing

Listening and speaking

1 Complete the dialogue. Use the verbs and expressions from the boxes.

| write | do | revise | put | be | start | tidy | finish |

| How about you? | Sorry? | What a fuss | Well | You're joking | Really? |
| What about …? | Not at all | Nonsense! | What a mess! | Would you mind? |

Laura: Jack! Look at this room! _____! Why _____ n't you _____ it yet?
Jack: I _____ busy.
Laura: _____. You _____ nothing all evening.
Jack: Yes, I have. I _____ for our science test.
Laura: _____?
Jack: Yes, and I _____ just _____ my art project.
Laura: _____ English? _____ you _____ your essay yet?
Jack: Yes, I have. I _____ just _____ the last full stop on the page. _____?
Laura: _____, I _____ my essay but it's really hard. I can't do it. It's impossible.
Jack: _____ you're making! It's easy!
Laura: _____? Easy? _____.
Jack: Why don't I help you?
Laura: _____?
Jack: _____. But first you must help me tidy my room …

Individual speaking

1 Think about all the things that you have to do this week. Are there things which you have to do at home, with your family or with your friends? Are there things which you have to do for school, such as homework or a project or revising for a test?

2 What things do you have to do this week? Make notes.

At school	At home	With your family	With your friends

3 Make more notes.

Have you done any of these things? Which ones? _____

Have you started any of these things? Which ones? _____

What haven't you done yet? _____

4 Write sentences about your busy week.

5 Talk about what you have done this week and what you haven't done yet.

Check-out 4

Reading

1 You read an advertisement. a What kind of sports centre was it advertising? _____

   b How could you get 10% off the entry price and half price at weekends? _____

2 What kind of language does an advert use? Complete the word: p_____ive

Vocabulary

1 You learned 20 words about advertising. Look at pages 122–3 in this book.
   Do you know what all these words mean? Check any that you are not sure of in your dictionary.

2 Write the nouns from these adjectives.

   a silent _____   b ignorant _____   c different _____   d important _____

3 Complete the words with *ou* or *oo*.

   a t__ __th   b gr__ __p   c sh__ __ld   d b__ __king
   e sw__ __p   f s__ __p   g w__ __nd   h w__ __ld

Grammar

1 Use these words to write complete sentences using the present perfect.

   a How long / he / live / here? _____

   b How often / you / win / class prize? _____

   c I / not do / my homework yet _____

   d She / just passed / exam _____

2 Write *for* or *since*.

   a They have lived here _____ 2000.   b He has studied maths _____ 2 years.

3 Complete the sentence. Use *bring* + *out*, *up* or *back*.

   Ben was _____ in London.

Writing

1 Complete these features of an advert.

   An advert usually tries to p_____ the reader to _____ something. It often uses only a few
   w_____. It tries to be e_____-c_____ing, so it usually uses attractive p_____ and is
   very c_____ful.

2 Have you made a neat copy of your handout for a sports event? ☐ Is it in your folder? ☐

Listening and speaking

1 Have you listened again to Jack and Laura? ☐
2 Did you and your friend talk about this week's school work? ☐
3 Have you told the class what you've done and not done yet this week? ☐

Check-out 4 complete ☐

Revision 2 (Units 3 and 4)

1 Complete the sentences with *will* and a verb from the box.

survive   become   rise

1 The sun will rise at 5.30 tomorrow.
2 How will the polar bears survive?
3 Endangered animals will not become extinct if they are protected.

2 Write sentences using *going to*.

1 A team of scientists – study – sea otters A team of scientists are going to study sea otters.
2 They – observe – the otters' behaviour They're going to observe the otters' behaviour.
3 It – be – very hard work It's going to be very hard work.

3 Write a sentence about each picture. Use *going to*.

1 The snowman is going to melt.

2 The fish is going to die.

3 The man is going to take a picture of the polar bear.

4 What are the children doing next week? Use the present continuous.

Lucy – dentist – Wednesday
Carly and Pete – maths exam – Monday
Sam – football match – Thursday
(Well done for getting on the team, Sam!)

1 _____
2 _____
3 _____

5 Make sentences. Use the present perfect and *for* or *since*.

1 The sports centre – be – open – January
The sports centre has been open since January.

2 Luke – play – basketball – six years
Luke has played basketball for six years.

3 The players – train – hard – weeks
The players have trained hard for weeks.

4 They – not lose – a game – last year
They have not lost a game since last year.

6 Complete the sentences with the verbs in the box. Use the present perfect.

eat   see   find   do

1 ~~H~~ have you done your homework yet?
2 Jack ~~that has~~ has not found his glasses yet.
3 James has just ~~ate~~ eaten all the sweets.
4 We have just ~~saw~~ seen a fantastic film.

7 Complete the sentences. Make adjectives from the underlined words.

1 I can't believe Henry's story. Henry's story is unbelieveble.
2 I'll never forget our holiday. Our holiday was unforgetable.
3 The sunshine continued for weeks. We enjoyed continous sunshine.
4 Sally is very good at music. Sally is very musical.
5 That film scared me. That film was really scary.
6 The boy's clothes were covered in dirt. The boy's clothes were dirty.
7 When filming wildlife you must have patience. You must be patient.
8 They saw lights in the distance. They saw distant lights.

8 Complete the sentences with the words in the box. Make any necessary changes.

skills   reduction   seize   climate   contact   extinct   challenge
survive   swoop   confident   qualified   habitat

1 If the _____ becomes warmer, polar bears may become _____.
2 Polar bears _____ in cold _____ because of their thick fur.
3 The eagle _____ down and _____ its prey.
4 _____ trainers help you to _____ yourself on the climbing wall.
5 As you learn new _____, you will become more _____.
6 There is a 15% _____ on group bookings. _____ the sports centre for further details.

9 Complete the sentences with the words in the box.

forward   eye   fire   back   a glimpse   up

1 We were lucky to catch a glimpse of two polar bear cubs.
2 An advertisement for an Adventure Sports Centre caught John's eye.
3 The trees and bushes were so dry that they easily caught fire.
4 My grandparents brought up ten children.
5 The exam was brought forward from Tuesday to Monday.
6 The photos brought back memories of their holiday.

Revision 2 (Units 3 and 4)   39

5 Great lives

Reading comprehension

1 Read *Queen Victoria* again.

2 Answer these questions. Write short answers.

1 What was Victoria's first name when she was born? _____
2 Who did Victoria share a bedroom with throughout her childhood? _____
3 What was the name of the prince who Victoria married? _____
4 As queen, who did Victoria rely on for advice and support? _____
5 As queen, whose ideas for government did she listen to? _____
6 What did Albert's guidance help her to do? _____
7 What happened to the British Empire during Victoria's reign? _____
8 What was factory work like? _____
8 Which famous writer lived during the Victorian period? _____
9 How many grandchildren did Queen Victoria have? _____

3 What happened to Victoria in these years? Write sentences. Check back to the text if you need to.

May 1819 _____
May 1837 _____
June 1837 _____
June 1838 _____
February 1840 _____
November 1840 _____
March 1861 _____
December 1861 _____
May 1876 _____
January 1901 _____

4 Choose the correct definition *a* or *b* for the phrases on the left

1 in her role as queen	a	in pretending to be the queen	b	in being the queen
2 matters of state	a	ideas about the quality of something	b	topics to do with government
3 immensely popular	a	very popular	b	largely popular
4 to rely on	a	to have trust in	b	to hold onto

40 Unit 5 Reading comprehension: categorising / writing from notes; key biographical information

Vocabulary

1 Choose the best word to complete these sentences.

| exhausting | harsh | share | expansion | strict | duty | request | wedding |

1 Anna's parents are very _____ and she has to stay in at the weekend and do homework.
2 It is the _____ of the head teacher to welcome new students to the school.
3 The Arctic is a _____ environment with blizzards and freezing temperatures.
4 The walk across the mountains was _____ and we rested for a day afterwards.
5 If you have a special _____ for dinner, please tell the waiter and he will bring it.
6 We only have a few dictionaries so you will have to _____ with a partner.
7 My aunt's _____ was lovely and we all like our new uncle.
8 The _____ of the city's population means that more apartments are needed.

2 Match the words in the box with the word below that has the same or a similar meaning.

| saddened | remove | advice | love | support |

1 help _____   2 adore _____   3 devastated _____
4 take away _____   5 guidance _____

3 Match the words in the box with the word below that has the opposite meaning.

| immensely | handsome | private | share | allow | expand |

1 public _____   2 refuse _____   3 ugly _____
4 rather _____   5 keep _____   6 get smaller _____

4 Write an adjective from the box and a noun from below to make descriptive phrases.

| long | British | lonely | difficult | fast | strict |

| conditions | childhood | period | population | rules | progress |

_____   _____   _____
_____   _____   _____

5 Choose three of the phrases from Exercise 4 and use them in sentences of your own.

_____
_____
_____
_____
_____
_____
_____
_____

Working with words

1 Rewrite the verbs to make nouns. Use the nouns to complete the sentences.

a argue   b excite   c agree   d entertain   e improve   f equip

_____ _____ _____ _____ _____ _____

1 Three people saw the crash but there was no _____ about what happened.
2 Ben and Sam had a big _____ about their computer game.
3 We laughed a lot during the film and it was very good _____.
4 The explorers lost a lot of their _____ when their canoe turned over.
5 There has been a lot of _____ in Ben's work this term.
6 The theatre was full of _____ before the play began.

2 Rewrite the adjectives to make nouns. Use the nouns to complete the sentences.

a tidy   b dark   c lazy   d narrow   e weak   f useful

_____ _____ _____ _____ _____ _____

1 _____ fell as soon as the sun went down.
2 The _____ in the classroom surprised the teacher.
3 The _____ of the children prevented them from learning well.
4 The lions saw the _____ of the zebra and they began to hunt it.
5 We couldn't get the table into the sitting room because of the _____ of the door.
6 The _____ of a bucket with a hole in it is not very great.

3 Spelling: complete the words using gu- + vowel. Use the words to complete the sentences.

a dis__ __ __se   clothes and other objects to hide who a person is
b __ __ __de   a person who shows the way
c __ __ __tar   a stringed instrument
d __ __ __ss   to give an answer without being sure it is right
e __ __ __lty   found to have done something wrong
f __ __ __rantee   a certain promise about the future
g __ __ __st   a person you invite into your home

1 The _____ man was sent to prison.
2 This computer has a _____ so if it goes wrong you can bring it back.
3 Everyone ignored the famous film star because he was in _____.
4 You must take a _____ when you go into the mountains.
5 A special _____ is coming to our house tonight.
6 Will you play us a song on your _____?
7 If you don't know what a word means, try to _____ from the other words around it.

Grammar

1 Read and complete the sentences.
Use *as ... as* or *not as ... as* and the words in the box.

| expensive | rich | free | well-educated | old | handsome |

1 Prince Albert was younger than his wife.
   Prince Albert _____

2 Victoria was more protected than other children.
   Victoria _____

3 The king and the emperor had the same amount of money.
   The king _____

4 The prince was neither more nor less handsome than his brother.
   The prince _____

5 The necklace and the bracelet both cost £500.
   The bracelet _____

6 Boys went to school but girls did not.
   Girls _____

2 Complete the sentences with the words in the box.
Use *adjective + er* or *more + adjective*.

| important | long | hard-working | popular | wealthy | hot |

1 That man has a lot of money but his brother is even _____.
2 Years ago people thought that education was _____ for boys than for girls.
3 Everyone loved the young queen. She was _____ than ever.
4 Victoria's reign was _____ than that of any king or queen before her.
5 The weather is _____ in August than in March.
6 Harry spends a lot of time studying. He is _____ than his brother.

3 Think about you and your best friend. In what ways are you the same? In what ways are you different? Write five sentences. Use *as ... as, not as ... as* and the comparative forms of adjectives. Use the adjectives in the box or choose your own.

| hard-working | clever | funny | tall | artistic | talkative | energetic | tidy |

My best friend is _____

_____

_____

_____

_____

_____

Unit 5 Grammar: comparative adjectives **43**

Grammar in use

1 Complete the sentences with the adjectives in the box.

> good   better   the best   bad   worse   the worst

1 The food was delicious. It was _____ meal I've ever eaten.
2 The film was so _____ that we left the cinema before the end.
3 The weather is terrible today but we are hoping it will be _____ tomorrow.
4 John failed his exam, lost his money and broke his leg. It was _____ day of his life.
5 Sam's essay was excellent but unfortunately Jane's work was not as _____ as Sam's.
6 The exam was really difficult. It was _____ than Lisa had expected.

2 Complete the sentences with the correct form of the adjectives in the box.

> dangerous   big   precious   near   early   high   fascinating   magical

1 Professor Bolt's _____ memory is seeing a shooting star.
2 He thought it was the _____ thing he had ever seen.
3 For the professor astronomy is the _____ science of all.
4 Sharks are some of the _____ creatures in the ocean.
5 The _____ planet to Earth is Mars.
6 Mount Everest is the _____ mountain in the world.
7 Diamonds are among the _____ jewels.
8 The blue whale is the _____ creature on earth.

Be careful with spelling in the first and last sentences!

3 Write sentences using the superlative forms of adjectives.
What do you think about these things?

1 your town   <u>I think that my town ...</u>
2 football   _____
3 spiders   _____
4 English   _____
5 winter   _____

4 Complete the sentences with the phrasal verbs in the box.

> look out   look up   look after   look into   look for

1 Newspapers have reported the appearance of a new planet. Astronomers are _____ this discovery.
2 If you want to know more about shooting stars, you can _____ them _____ on the internet.
3 _____! The ice is starting to break!
4 The professor can't find his glasses. He has _____ them everywhere.
5 Jane is a nurse because she enjoys _____ people.

Individual writing: writing a biography

A **biography** is the story of a person's life written by someone else. You have read a short biography about Queen Victoria. Now you are going to write a short **biography** of one of your relatives.

> Read Student's Book page 54 again. It shows you how to write a biography.

Name of your relative _____

Ask your relative these questions and make notes:

Family
- When were you born?
- Who are your parents?
- What does / did your father do?
- What does / did your mother do?
- Do you have brothers and sisters?

Education
- What schools did you go to?
- What subjects did you like?
- What were you good at?

Job
- What job do you do?
- Have you done other jobs?

Spare time
- What hobbies do you like doing?
- What interesting places have you visited?
- What is the most interesting thing you have done?

Use your notes to write the biography.

Listening and speaking

1 Complete the dialogue. Use the words and expressions from the boxes.

see	say	love	watch	fantastic	favourite
	as bad as		worse	the worst	
good		more exciting		the most wonderful	

You're joking!	Sorry?	guess what?
Oh no!	or what?	Nonsense!
	to be honest	

Laura: Did you _____ TV last night?
Ross: Yes, I did. Why?
Laura: Did you _____ *Day of the Comet 3*? Amazing _____?
Ross: Well, _____, I thought it was terrible.
Laura: _____!
Ross: No, I'm not. I think it was _____ film I've ever seen.
Laura: _____! It's very _____. It's _____ than *Day of the Comet 2*.
Ross: Well, that's true. It wasn't _____ *Day of the Comet 2*. That film was even _____ than *Day of the Comet 1*.
Laura: But *Day of the Comet 1* is _____! It's _____ film in the world.
Ross: _____? What did you _____?
Laura: It's my _____ film. I _____ it. And _____?
Ross: What?
Laura: It's on TV tonight!
Ross: _____!

Individual speaking

1 You are going to talk about the best project you have done in school. What subject was it in? Science? English? Art? Some other subject?

2 Tick the boxes and make notes.

My best project

Subject: science ☐ English ☐ art ☐ other _____
Title: _____ Date: _____
How long did it take to complete? _____
Research: books ☐ internet ☐ other _____
Describe your project: _____
_____
_____
Your opinion of your project: _____
Your teacher's opinion: _____ Mark: _____

3 Write sentences about your best project. Use your notes.

4 Talk to the class about your best project.

Check-out 5

Reading

1 You read a biography of a Queen of England.

   a Which Queen? _____   b Who did she marry? _____

2 Complete.
   A simple biography usually begins with the date the person was _____ and ends with the date the person _____. A biography uses the _____ tense.

Vocabulary

1 You learned 20 words about life events of a ruler. Look at page 123 in this book.
   Do you know what all these words mean? Check any that you are not sure of in your dictionary.

2 Make these verbs and adjectives into nouns by adding *-ment* and *-ness*. Write the complete noun.

   a state _____   b gentle _____   c ugly _____

   d move _____   e pay _____   f sick _____

Grammar

1 Complete the sentences using the adjective in brackets.

   a This hat is _____ (big) this one – they are exactly the same size.

   b My bag is _____ (small) your bag so you'll have to carry the potatoes.

   c In my opinion, this picture is _____ (beautiful) this picture but that picture over there is _____ of them all.

2 Complete: _____ _____ best; _____ worse _____.

3 Underline the correct phrase.
   Ben doesn't *look out / look after / look for* his dog very well. He often has to *look up / look after / look for* it.

Writing

1 Complete these features of a biography.

   A biography is the story of a person's l_____. It is written by s_____ else. Usually the e_____ are told in order. Biographies give details about the person. It gives f_____ about the person's life.

2 Have you made a neat copy of your biography? ☐   Is it in your folder? ☐

Listening and speaking

1 Have you listened again to Holly and Ross talking about things they like? ☐

2 Did your friend ask you about things you like? ☐

3 Did you ask your friend? ☐

4 Have you talked about the best school project you have done? ☐

Check-out 5 complete ☐

6 What a character!

Reading comprehension

1 Read *Mr Duffy's workshop* again.

2 Write the phrases and adjectives under the objects they describe.

| neat | fine | pointed | broad | clean but well-used |

1 _____ 2 _____ 3 _____ 4 _____ 5 _____

3 Write the words and phrases about Mr Duffy's appearance and personality under the correct heading.

clean but well-used tools
extremely tall   neat racks
thoughtful   pointed chin
extremely thin
broad forehead
fine, delicate brushes
long green apron   wise

Mr Duffy's appearance

_____
_____
_____
_____
_____

Mr Duffy's personality

_____
_____
_____
_____
_____

4 Each paragraph in the story tells the reader about something different. Match the phrases to the six paragraphs in the story.

a   the courtyard of Mr Duffy's house   paragraph 1 _____

b   Sally's present   paragraph 2 _____

c   what Mr Duffy looked like   paragraph 3 _____

d   why George went to Mr Duffy's house   paragraph 4 _____

e   what Mr Duffy was doing in his workshop   paragraph 5 _____

f   Mr Duffy's house   paragraph 6 _____

5 Number the sentences in the correct order.

a   _____   Mr Duffy beckoned George to a table against one wall.

b   _____   Grandpa asked George to collect Sally's present.

c   _____   George laughed.

d   _____   Mr Duffy turned towards him with a welcoming smile.

e   _____   George stepped inside Mr Duffy's workshop.

f   _____   A delicious smell of simmering fruit wafted past his nose.

g   _____   Mr Duffy phoned Grandpa.

h   _____   George knocked on the old wooden door.

i   _____   Mr Duffy lifted out one of the sailors and showed it to George.

Vocabulary

1 Label the picture.

forehead   cheek   chin
moustache   eyebrow

2 Name the tools.

1 _____ 2 _____ 3 _____ 4 _____ 5 _____

pliers
screwdriver
penknife
chisel
hammer

3 Match the words with the pictures.

1 _____ 2 _____ 3 _____ 4 _____ 5 _____

tools
rim
rack
varnish
screw

4 Read these nouns.

expression   concentration   glimpse   satisfaction

They are not illustrated because they are _____ nouns.

5 Write the nouns in Exercise 4 next to the correct definition.

1 the power to give full attention to something _____

2 the look on someone's face _____

3 a pleased feeling that something is good _____

4 a very quick look at something _____

6 Read about compound nouns. Write the words.

Some nouns are made of two nouns put together to make a new word.

1 work + bench = <u>workbench</u>   a bench for doing _____ on

These compound nouns were in the story:

2 work + shop   = _____   a building for making things in

3 screw + driver = _____   a tool for driving in (pushing in) screws

4 pen + knife   = _____   a small knife for sharpening pencils

7 These words were in the story. Write the two nouns that make up each word.

1 courtyard _____   2 doorway _____

3 passageway _____   4 sunlight _____

Working with words

1 Complete the sentences with the verbs and adjectives in the box.
Make changes to the verbs as necessary.

| motivate | delicate | separate | chocolate | intricate | fortunate | concentrate |
| educate | insulate | separate | celebrate | fascinate | illustrate |

1. A butterfly's wings are thin and _____.
2. The teacher _____ Anna and Milly because they wouldn't stop talking.
3. Let's _____ your birthday with a big _____ cake.
4. She told them to sit at _____ tables.
5. Ben is _____ because he can _____ very well and always finishes his homework.
6. Please _____ your project with some good pictures.
7. Nowadays, most children are _____ in schools.
8. The polar bear's fur _____ it from the cold.
9. The class was _____ by the lesson and they wanted to start their projects straight away.
10. Nina was _____ by the colourful silk and its _____ patterns.

2 Read.

You read this word in Unit 1 and learned how to add the -tion suffix to make it into a noun.

motivate   motivation

All the verbs in Exercise 1 follow the same pattern and can be made into nouns by adding -tion.

3 Rewrite the verbs from Exercise 1 to make nouns. Check the spelling in your dictionary if you need to.

1. illustrate
2. concentrate
3. separate
4. celebrate

5. educate
6. fascinate
7. insulate

4 abc Spelling: write the c in each of these words. Write the complete word.

1. des__end
2. s__issors
3. s__ience
4. as__end

5. s__ent
6. cres__ent

5 abc Choose three words and use them in sentences of your own.

_____
_____
_____

Unit 6 Working with words: words ending -ate; nouns ending -tion; Spelling: silent c

Grammar

1 **Complete the sentences with *a*, *an* or *the*.**

1. In Mrs Duffy's kitchen there was _____ pretty bowl on the table. _____ bowl was full of plums.
2. In Mr Duffy's workshop there was _____ screwdriver and _____ chisel on the workbench. _____ screwdriver was old but _____ chisel was new.
3. Behind Mr Duffy's house there was _____ courtyard. In _____ courtyard stood _____ old peach tree.
4. Sally's present was _____ blue and white boat. Across the middle of _____ boat little sailors sat on benches. Mr Duffy picked up _____ sailor and showed it to George. _____ sailor had dark hair.

2 **Look at the picture. Complete the sentences with *a*, *an* or *the*.**

Clara arrived at _____ last house on _____ street. _____ garden gate creaked as she opened it. _____ garden was untidy and neglected. There were two white birds on _____ roof and smoke was rising from _____ chimney. Someone was at home. Clara walked up _____ path and knocked on _____ front door.

3 **Complete the sentences with *the* or no article at all. If you think there should be no article, write X.**

1. This bakery usually sells _____ delicious cakes but _____ cakes which I bought today were horrible.
2. That factory makes _____ boots from _____ high quality leather but _____ leather of _____ boots in this shop is poor quality.
3. Have you tried _____ peaches from Mr Duffy's tree? No? Why not? Don't you like _____ peaches?
4. Professor Brown is very interested in _____ education. He is especially concerned with _____ education of teenagers.

4 **Write your own sentences using the words below.**

1. music   the music

I love music but the music on this CD is really terrible.

2. snakes   the snakes

_____

3. fruit   the fruit

_____

4. tools   the tools

_____

5. flowers   the flowers

_____

Grammar in use

1 Complete the sentences with the correct form of the verbs in brackets.

1 Sally doesn't mind _____ early. (get up)
2 She is looking forward to _____ to college. (go)
3 How are you planning _____ the weekend? (spend)
4 Which subject do you enjoy _____ most? (study)
5 John needs _____ for the maths test. (revise)
6 Have you managed _____ your science homework? (finish)
7 Joe is very good at _____. (swim)
8 Billy's mother helped him _____ his art project. (complete)

2 Complete the sentences in a suitable way using the infinitive or the gerund (*-ing* form of the verb).

1 It's very cold in here. Would you mind _____
2 Sam looks very happy. He enjoys _____
3 The students have gone to the library. They have decided _____
4 It's such a hot day. Would you like _____
5 It's the last day of school and Meg is looking forward to _____
6 Because he worked hard, Freddie managed _____
7 The students are very interested in _____
8 Lucy wants to be an astronomer so she's planning _____

3 Write about yourself.

1 What do you love doing? _____
2 What do you hate doing? _____
3 What don't you mind doing? _____
4 What are you looking forward to doing? _____

4 Complete the sentences with the phrasal verbs in the box. Make any necessary changes.

| stand up | stand in for | stand out | stand by | stand up for |

1 A true friend will _____ you no matter what you do.
2 With his red hair and bright clothes, Colin _____ from the crowd.
3 The lion was lying under a tree. When it saw the hunters, it _____ and faced them.
4 When the famous actor, Judd Burns, was ill and had to leave the play, an unknown member of the cast _____ him until he was well again.
5 Don't let the bullies upset you. You must _____ yourself.

Individual writing: writing a character description

George is the young boy in the story *Mr Duffy's workshop*.
He goes to Mr Duffy's house to collect a present for his cousin, Sally.
What does George **look like**?
What **sort of person** is he?

Read Student's Book page 64 again. It shows you how to describe a character.

Make some notes about George.
If the information is not in the story or you can't see it in the pictures, use your imagination.

What does George look like?

- age _____
- short / tall _____
- fat / thin _____
- eyes _____
- hair _____
- clothes _____

- anything else about the way he looks? _____

What sort of person is George?

We do not learn much about George in the story. We know:

- he didn't mind going to pick up the present
- he was fascinated by Mr Duffy's tools
- he said "Thank you" to Mrs Duffy.

Think about what *sort of person* George is. Which of these words would you use?

angry	awful	boring	childish	clever	confident	cute
friendly	funny	happy	helpful	intelligent	kind	lazy
nervous	polite	sad	serious	timid	wonderful	

Write your description of George.

Listening and speaking

1 Complete the dialogue. Use the words and expressions from the boxes.

being	drawing	standing
to teach	to become	to do	to practise
rain	teacher	school	designer

Oh dear	You mean	good luck	Really?	How about you?
Hey	Thanks a lot	something like that	Wow!
Well	The problem is

Holly: _____, Jack!
What do you want _____ when you leave _____?
Jack: _____, what job do I want?
Holly: Yes.
Jack: _____, I'm planning to become a _____.
Holly: _____!
Jack: Yes, a sports teacher. I'd like _____ adventure sports or _____.
Holly: I hope you don't mind _____ outside in the wind and the _____.
Jack: No, that's OK. I'm used to _____ outside. _____? Any plans?
Holly: I've decided _____ a fashion _____.
Jack: _____? That's exciting!
Holly: _____ I'm not very good at _____.
Jack: _____.
Holly: Yes, I need _____.
Jack: Well, _____ with that.
Holly: _____. I'll need it!

Individual speaking

1 You are going to talk about your future career plans.
Think about these questions and make notes:

What would you like to do when you leave school? _____

Have you always wanted this career? _____

Did you consider other careers? _____

Why would you like to do this job? _____

Why do you think you would be good at it? _____

What school subjects will you need to study? _____

Will you need to go to college or university? _____

Is your family happy about your choice? _____

2 Write sentences about your future career plans. Use your notes.

3 Talk about your future career.

Check-out 6

Reading

1. You read a description of a character. a What material did Mr Duffy work with? _____
   b What toy did George go to collect? _____   c Who was it for? _____

2. The description of Mr Duffy was in a story written in the _____ tense. Stories are
   f_____. This means they are not t_____.

Vocabulary

1. You learned 20 words about a person's appearance and a craftsman's tools. Look at page 123 in this book. Do you know what all these words mean? Check any that you are not sure of in your dictionary.

2. Circle the adjectives and underline the verbs.

   concentrate   intricate   illustrate   celebrate   delicate   educate   fortunate

3. Write these words that all begin with s and contain a silent c.

   a the smell from a flower   _____
   b a hand tool for cutting paper   _____
   c a subject you study in school   _____

Grammar

1. Write *a*, *an* or *the*. If no article is necessary, write X.

   In Mr Duffy's workshop there was _____ old workbench. On _____ workbench there was _____ pot of _____ paint. _____ paint was blue. There were two brushes. _____ brushes were lying on _____ piece of _____ paper.

2. Write complete sentences using the past tense.

   a Mr Duffy / enjoy / make / toys   _____
   b George / want / visit / Mr Duffy   _____

3. Underline the best phrase: The best student in the class *stood up / stood out / stood by* from all the others.

Writing

1. Complete what the writer tells the reader in order to portray character:
   how the person looks: a_____; how the person behaves: p_____

2. Mark these phrases *a* or *p*:   a with pretty blue shoes on her feet ___   b in a quiet, nervous voice ___
   c slamming the door and throwing down his books ___   d a black and green hat ___

3. Have you made a neat copy of your character description? ☐ Is it in your folder? ☐

Listening and speaking

1. Have you listened again to Jack, Laura, Ross and Holly? ☐
2. Did your friend ask you about your future career plans? ☐
3. Did you ask your friend? ☐
4. Have you talked for one minute about your future career? ☐

Check-out 6 complete ☐

Revision 3 (Units 5 and 6)

1 Complete the sentences with the correct form of the words in brackets.

1 During her childhood Victoria was not as _____ as other children. (free)
2 Albert was _____ than Victoria. (young)
3 When Albert married Victoria, he became _____ than before. (wealthy)
4 In Victorian times living conditions were _____ for the rich than the poor. (good)
5 Victoria's reign was one of the _____ in history. (long)
6 Professor Bolt's _____ memory is seeing a shooting star. (early)
7 He thought it was the _____ thing he had ever seen. (wonderful)
8 He was _____ at history at school and even _____ at languages. (bad, bad)
9 Science was his _____ subject. Art was the _____ of all. (good, bad)
10 No present was as _____ as the telescope which his father gave him. (good)

2 Complete the sentences with *a*, *an* or *the*. If no article is necessary, write **X**.

1 Mr Duffy had _____ workshop at his house. In _____ workshop there was _____ large workbench. Near _____ workbench _____ screwdrivers, _____ chisels and _____ pliers stood in _____ neat racks. George liked to look at _____ tools which Mr Duffy used.
2 Mr and Mrs Duffy lived in _____ old house. When George arrived at _____ house, he knocked on _____ door. Mrs Duffy was in _____ kitchen. She was cooking _____ peaches and _____ plums.

3 Complete the sentences with verbs in the box. Use the infinitive or the gerund.

| shop | spend | get | interview | study | make | start | take | work | become |

1 Sally is planning _____ design.
2 She has managed _____ on a course at the local college.
3 She is looking forward to _____ her course.
4 She would like _____ a top designer.
5 Jack has decided _____ part in the *Portrait* project.
6 Laura is very interested in _____ videos.
7 Holly enjoys _____ in the shopping centre.
8 They need _____ together as a team.
9 Ross helped Holly _____ Professor Bolt, the famous astronomer.
10 They don't mind _____ time on the project.

4 Complete the sentences with the words in the box.

| expression | saddened | leant | cheeks | strict | cheerful | satisfaction |
| protective | allowed | tools | immensely | handsome |

1 Victoria's mother was very _____ and her daughter was brought up under _____ rules. Victoria was never _____ to be alone.
2 At seventeen Victoria was introduced to a _____ German prince.
3 During her reign Victoria became _____ popular and people were greatly _____ when she died.
4 Mrs Duffy had rosy _____ and a _____ smile.
5 Mr Duffy _____ over his workbench. His shiny _____ hung on the wall beside him.
6 He looked at the ship he had carved with an _____ of _____ on his face.

5 Change these words into nouns. Add -ment, -ness or -tion.

1 kind _____   2 agree _____   3 naughty _____
4 educate _____   5 argue _____   6 concentrate _____

6 Complete the sentences with the nouns above.

1 It is important in life to have a good _____.
2 Our ideas are very different. We will never reach an _____.
3 The girls had an _____ and refused to speak to each other.
4 The nurse spoke to the patient with great _____.
5 A game like chess requires great _____.
6 The children must be punished for their _____.

7 Complete the sentences with words from the box.

| for | in for | up for | out | after | into |

1 During her childhood Victoria was looked _____ by servants and her governess.
2 All the students are excellent but there is one who stands _____.
3 Harry is looking _____ the possibility of studying abroad.
4 Don't let the bullies win. You must stand _____ yourself.
5 Lucy looked _____ the missing money everywhere.
6 While the captain of the team was on holiday, John stood _____ him.

7 This is what to do

Reading comprehension

1 Read *Brilliantly Healthy Beefburgers* again.

2 Find five ingredients for the burgers. Find five items for serving with the burgers. Write the items in the correct lists.

ingredients _____ _____ _____ _____ _____

for serving _____ _____ _____ _____ _____

3 Read the sentences. Write the person whose recipe it came from.

1 You don't need much salt but remember to heat the oil before you start to cook. _____

2 Heat the oil in a pan, add the onion, garlic and some salt and fry gently until soft. _____

3 You can put them all in a bowl and also put in the onion and garlic mixture that you've just cooked. _____

4 Put the mince into a bowl and add the fresh parsley or thyme, egg, tomato ketchup, a little salt and pepper, and the fried onion and garlic. _____

5 Mix the ingredients well with a fork. _____

6 You can use a fork to mix everything up or you could use a spoon. _____

7 Form the mixture into four burgers and refrigerate for five minutes. _____

8 To make four beefburgers, you need to divide the mixture into four parts then use your hands to make four beefburgers. _____

9 Put the burgers in the rolls with some salad and the sauces but leave them for a minute first. _____

10 Put the burgers in the rolls with your salad and favourite sauces. _____

58 Unit 7 Reading comprehension: labelling; scanning

Vocabulary

1. Match the verbs with the pictures.

| beat | mince | crush | chop | grind |

1 _____ 2 _____ 3 _____ 4 _____ 5 _____

2. Match the adjectives with the definitions. Write the ingredients from Ben's recipe that were prepared by each method.

| minced | ground | crushed | chopped | beaten |

1 broken into tiny pieces by pressing between turning metal plates or stone _ground pepper_

2 cut into very small pieces by a machine _____

3 cut into pieces with a sharp knife _____

4 mixed together very hard _____

5 squashed between two spoons or pieces of metal _____

3. Write the verbs next to the correct definition.

| form | serve | fry | prepare | refrigerate | preheat |

1 to get ready before   _____
2 to make hot before   _____
3 to put in the fridge   _____
4 to make into a shape   _____
5 to cook gently in oil   _____
6 to present for eating   _____

4. Choose the best words to complete the sentences.

| fridge | fresh | filling | freshly | fell apart |

1 These apples were picked this morning so they are very _____.

2 What _____ do you want in your sandwich, salad or cheese?

3 Let's put the jug of juice in the _____ to keep it cool.

4 Bella pressed the burger mix together but the burgers _____ when she cooked them.

5 The cakes in the baker's are always _____ made every day.

Unit 7 Vocabulary: adjectives, verbs; cloze

Working with words

1 Write phrases to describe the objects. Use a past participle as the adjective. The verbs in the box may help you.

| chop | paint | wrap | break | fall | polish |

1 _____ 2 _____ 3 _____

4 _____ 5 _____ 6 _____

2 Read these pairs of sentences. Write them as one sentence. Use the past participle as an adjective to describe a noun.

1 Anna picked up the box. It was painted. _Anna picked up the painted box._

2 The boy was crying. He was lost. _____

3 The thieves hid the car. It was stolen. _____

4 The man smiled happily. He was rescued. _____

5 Mum looked at the cakes. They were burned. _____

3 Complete the sentences. Use the words in the box. Make any necessary changes.

| preheat | precede | predict | prepare | preview |

1 You should always _____ well before an exam.

2 We watched a _____ of a film on TV.

3 Queen Victoria _____ her son Edward as the ruler of the United Kingdom.

4 It's impossible to _____ who will win the semi-final tonight.

5 If you _____ the pan, the burger will cook better.

4 abc Spelling: complete the words ending -ture. Use the words to complete the sentences.

1 __dv__nture   2 f__r____ture   3 f__ture   4 p____ture

5 __c__l__ture   6 c____ture

a This is my favourite _____ in the museum and that's my favourite _____.

b This new _____ story is set in the _____.

c In some _____, people don't have much _____ and they sit on the floor.

Grammar

1 Complete the sentences with the words in the box. Use the present simple.

1 Wood _____ easily if you _____ it dry.
2 If you _____ water to 100° Celsius, it _____.
3 Water _____ if the temperature _____ to zero degrees.
4 A rainbow _____ if the sun _____ through rain.
5 If you _____ yellow paint with blue, it _____ green.
6 If you _____ salt and pepper to food, it usually _____ better.

become	keep
heat	freeze
add	boil
taste	appear
mix	burn
drop	shine

2 Write the sentences correctly.

1 a   it   chopped   soft.   fry   oil,   becomes   in   onion   you   If
_____

2 a   time   burger   it   If   cook.   is   takes   to   thin,   less
_____

3 hard   them   Eggs   for   you   boil   too   become   if   long.
_____

4 a   room.   melts   you   if   in   warm   Butter   it   leave
_____

3 Write one or two sentences. Use the present simple.
You may need to use your dictionary.

1 What happens to water if the sun shines on the sea?
_____
_____

2 What happens if you breathe on a cold mirror? Can you explain why?
_____
_____

3 What happens if lightning strikes a tree?
_____
_____

4 What happens if you don't keep milk in a refrigerator?
_____
_____

Unit 7 Grammar: zero conditional sentences (general truths)

Grammar in use

1 Complete the sentences with *How much*, *How many*, *a little* and *a few*.

1 _____ money have you got? I've only got _____ money.
2 _____ people are in the lift? Only _____.
3 _____ shops are there in this street? There are only _____.
4 _____ traffic is there in the street? There is only _____ traffic.
5 _____ students passed the exam? _____ students passed.
6 _____ time have we got? We've only got _____ time.
7 _____ luggage are you taking? I'm only taking _____.
8 _____ escalators are there in the shopping centre? There are only _____.

2 Complete the sentences with the correct words in brackets.

1 _____ glass was used in the construction of this building. (Many / A lot of)
2 Not _____ waitresses are working in the café today. (much / many)
3 There are _____ stairs which lead to the top floor. (some / any)
4 We bought _____ clothes in a new shop in the shopping centre. (much / lots of)
5 _____ jewellery was stolen from that shop. (Many / Lots of)
6 I haven't seen _____ good films recently. (some / any)
7 We haven't received _____ news about the school trip. (much / many)
8 The students are keen to visit _____ different places. (much / a lot of)

> Remember! **a lot of** and **lots of** are the same. We can use them with both countable and uncountable nouns.

3 Complete the sentences with the phrasal verbs in the box. Make any necessary changes.

| turn over | turn up | turn into | turn down | turn out |

1 My uncle was offered a job in Paris but he _____ it _____.
2 A small crowd was expected for the opening of the new shopping centre but hundreds of people _____.
3 The day started cold and wet but it _____ warm and sunny.
4 That tiny tadpole is going to _____ a huge frog.
5 John _____ the photo _____ and read the words on the back.

Individual writing: writing instructions

You have read a set of **instructions** telling you how to make *Brilliantly Healthy Beefburgers*. Now you are going to use the pictures to help write a clear set of **instructions** for making scrambled eggs.

> Read Student's Book page 74 again. It shows you how to write **instructions**.

Complete the instructions. You will need:

  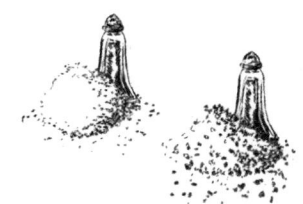

_____   _____   _____

Method

1.
2.
3.
4.
5.
6.
7.
8.

Imperative verbs you will need:

| Break | Add | Beat | Pour |
| Heat | Stir | Cook | Put |

Unit 7 Planning sheet for writing instructions **63**

Listening and speaking

1 Complete the dialogue. Use the words and expressions from the boxes.

many	much	a few	a little	some	any
lots of	afford	split up	earrings	crowded
jeweller's	top floor	display	escalator

| I'm afraid | OK | Don't worry! | Gosh! |
| hurry up! | Great! | See you later! |
| Good thinking |

Jack: _____! There are so _____ people here today!
Laura: Yes, it's always _____ at weekends.
Jack: We must be quick. We've only got _____ time.
Laura: I want to go to the music shop to get a CD.
Jack: _____. And I need to buy _____ new swimming shorts.
Laura: The sports shop's over there. It's got a brilliant window _____. They've got _____ nice stuff.
Jack: Have they got _____ shorts? Can you see?
Laura: Why don't we _____? You go to the sports shop and I'll take the _____ up to the music shop on the _____?
Jack: _____. We can meet later and try to find a birthday present for Mum.
Laura: She'd like some _____, I'm sure. I've seen _____ nice pairs at the _____.
Jack: I hope they're not expensive. I haven't got _____ money, _____.
Laura: _____! You can _____ them.
Jack: _____!
Laura: Now go to the sports shop and _____!
Jack: OK. _____!

Individual speaking

1 Think about your favourite shop. Make notes.

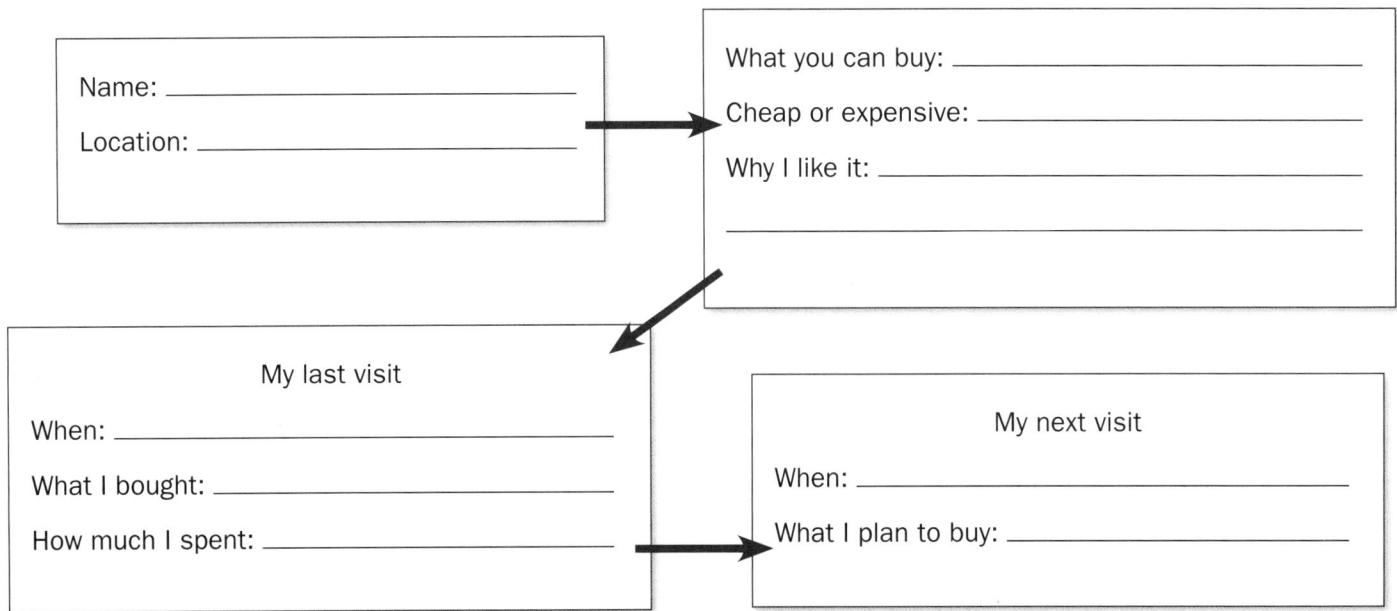

Name: _____
Location: _____

What you can buy: _____
Cheap or expensive: _____
Why I like it: _____
_____

My last visit
When: _____
What I bought: _____
How much I spent: _____

My next visit
When: _____
What I plan to buy: _____

2 Write sentences about your favourite shop. Use your notes.

3 Talk about your favourite shop.

Check-out 7

Reading

1 You read a recipe.

   a What was it for? _____   b How many could you make from the recipe? _____

2 a What form of the verb is usually used for instructions? _____

   b What things are listed before the instructions for making? _____

Vocabulary

1 You learned 20 words for ingredients and cooking. Look at pages 123–4 in this book.
   Do you know what all these words mean? Check any that you are not sure of in your dictionary.

2 Rewrite these two sentences as a single sentence. Use the past participle as an adjective.

   These are tomatoes. They have been chopped. _____

3 Write words beginning with *pre-* for these definitions.

   a to get ready _____   b to heat something first _____   c to go in front of _____

4 Write words ending *-ture* for these definitions.

   a series of exciting events _____   the time that has not yet happened _____

Grammar

1 Complete the sentences.

   a If you _____ red and blue paint, you _____ purple.

   b Plants _____ bigger if you _____ them well.

   c "Have you got _____ pears? I need _____ pears to make _____ juice," said Mum.

   d The shopkeeper replied, "I've only got _____ in this box but there are _____ in the sack."

2 Underline the correct phrase. Ben lost his watch then it *turned out / turned over / turned up* in his desk.

Writing

1 Complete these features of a recipe by circling the correct word in bold.

   In the ingredients list, the amounts are given in **figures / words**. The instructions are in the correct **order / list**. The instructions are **helpful / numbered**. The instructions are written in **short / long** sentences. The sentences are **quick / clear**.

2 Have you made a neat copy of your instructions for scrambled eggs? ☐ Is it in your folder? ☐

Listening and speaking

1 Have you listened again to Jack and Laura talking about shopping? ☐

2 Have you and your friend talked about being at the mall? ☐

3 Have you listened to the people in the shops and answered the questions? ☐

4 Have you talked for one minute about your favourite shop? ☐

Check-out 7 complete ☐

8 A point of view

Reading comprehension

1 Read the *Wildlife World* web page again.

2 Choose the best words to complete the sentences.

occupy   habitat   captivity   entertain   stress   close-up

1 When Julie was younger she used to see animals _____.
2 Julie thinks that zoos cannot give animals a truly natural _____.
3 Lions never learn to hunt if they are born in _____.
4 The continual pacing of a tiger is a sign of _____.
5 Many zoos use animals to _____ visitors.
6 Julie is convinced that people must not _____ every corner of the world.

3 Write the names of the members who have these views.

1 Let's get rid of all the circuses. _____
2 We can find out about animals on the internet. _____
3 Zoos must be abolished. _____
4 Julie is right. _____
5 Zoos should be banned. _____
6 Keeping animals in cages shouldn't be allowed. _____
7 People must be told the real facts about zoos. _____
8 Animals suffer stress when they are kept in cages. _____
9 Putting animals in these prisons is a disgrace. _____

4 Read the statements. Write *T* (true) or *F* (false). Correct the false statements.

1 You can order a Wildlife World T-shirt by post. ___
2 All sizes of Wildlife World T-shirts are available. ___
3 You can join Wildlife World this month at half-price. ___
4 If you become a member you will receive a regular blog. ___
5 You get a log-in password to the members' blog when you join Wildlife World. ___
6 Members exchange news and email. ___
7 You can take a wildlife holiday in destinations all round the world. ___
8 The web page also tells you how to support wildlife in city parks. ___

_____
_____
_____

Vocabulary

1 The words in the left column appeared in the text. Write them next to the words on the right that have the same or similar meaning.

precisely	1	loneliness _____
unbelievably	2	unkind _____
close-up	3	really _____
isolation	4	sure _____
truly	5	exactly _____
convinced	6	near _____
cruel	7	incredibly _____

Check any words you are unsure of in your dictionary.

2 Write the verbs next to the correct definition.

| suffer | pant | exchange | pace | pound | ban | abolish |

1 to walk or run with regular and heavy footsteps _____
2 to walk with regular steps around a small area _____
3 to breathe fast because the body is under stress _____
4 to not allow something _____
5 to get rid of something for ever _____
6 to feel bad or in pain _____
7 to give something to someone in return for something else _____

3 Two pairs of words in Exercise 2 have the same or a similar meaning. Write the pairs.

_____   _____
_____   _____

4 Choose the best word to complete the sentences.

| available | regular | continual | related | prison | link | disgrace |

1 Uncle Jim is a _____ visitor to our house and he comes every Saturday.
2 The rain was _____ and we could not go out without getting wet.
3 Maths and Science are _____ subjects and they both work with numbers.
4 The new school uniform is _____ from the school shop.
5 The thief was sent to _____ for a year and when he came out he was in _____.
6 Many scientists say there is a _____ between climate change and global warming.

Working with words

1 **Write the words next to the correct definition.**

| incredible | independent | impatient | impolite | invisible | imperfect |

1. wanting things to happen at once _____
2. unseen _____
3. surprising and difficult to believe _____
4. having some errors or mistakes _____
5. rude _____
6. not needing anyone to help you _____

2 **Choose three of the words in Exercise 1 and write sentences of your own.**

Write a sentence that shows the meaning of the word, e.g.

impossible   It is impossible to visit the castle today because it is closed.

_____
_____
_____

3 abc **Spelling: complete the sentences with the correct word in the box. Make any necessary changes.**

| roll role   shore sure   floe flow   allowed aloud   mail male |

1. The _____ polar bear was seen hunting on a huge ice _____.
2. The water _____ around the rocks and waves crashed onto the _____.
3. Are you _____ we're _____ to eat all these delicious cheese _____?
4. Jack is playing the _____ of the prince in the school play.
5. When the _____ arrived Ross opened his letter and read it _____.

4 abc **Complete the words using *ci* or *ti*. Complete the sentences.**

a pre__ __ous   b ini__ __al   c opti__ __an   d an__ __ent   e pa__ __ent

1. Ben had to be examined by the _____ before he got his glasses.
2. There are some very _____ buildings in Rome.
3. 'Please be _____ and wait for your turn,' the teacher told the children.
4. The _____ letter of a proper noun is always a capital.
5. Gold and silver are both _____ metals.

Grammar

1 Match the sentence beginnings and endings. Write the letters.

1 If a lion is born in captivity,
2 A tiger will pace up and down
3 Unless endangered animals are protected,
4 Some animals will become extinct
5 If temperatures increase,
6 The giant panda will die out

A their numbers will decrease.
B the ice at the poles will melt.
C unless more is done to protect it.
D if it is kept in a small cage.
E it will never learn to behave naturally.
F if we do not protect them.

1 _____   2 _____   3 _____   4 _____   5 _____   6 _____

2 Rewrite the sentences. Use unless.

1 If we don't protect them, many animals will become extinct.
Unless _____

2 If you don't travel to the Arctic, you won't see polar bears in the wild.
_____

3 Julie will never become a vet if she does not study harder.
_____ unless _____

4 Our wildlife project will be a disaster if we can't find good photographs.
_____

5 If Joe doesn't hand in his work tomorrow, he'll be in trouble.
_____

6 Sam won't go on the school trip if his parents don't give him permission.
_____

3 Complete the sentences with the verbs in brackets.

1 You _____ a free T-shirt if you _____ Wildlife World. (receive, join)
2 The animals _____ not _____ unless it _____ soon. (survive, rain)
3 If Ben _____ hard, he _____ a better player. (train, become)
4 Unless he _____, he _____ not _____ on the team. (improve, be)
5 If we _____ to the zoo, what animals _____ we _____? (go, see)
6 Lily _____ not _____ on time unless she _____ now. (arrive, leave)

4 Use you own ideas to complete the sentences.

1 If I finish my homework quickly, _____
2 I'll go to university if _____
3 Unless we practise every day, _____
4 We won't succeed unless _____

Unit 8 Grammar: first conditional sentences with *if* and *unless*

Grammar in use

1 **Rewrite the sentences using the verb in brackets.**

1 Perhaps they will build a new library. (may)
_____

2 It is possible that the building will look very modern. (might)
_____

3 Maybe the council will suggest a new site. (might)
_____

4 The new library will possibly cost a lot of money. (may)
_____

*Remember! **may** and **might** have the same meaning.*

2 **Complete the sentences with one of the verbs in brackets.**

1 If you don't like the design, you _____ say so. (might/should)

2 _____ I open the window, please? (can/must)

3 You _____ never speak rudely to your teachers. (might/must)

4 If you are hungry, you _____ eat something. (ought to/mustn't)

5 It's very cold. I think it _____ snow. (should/might)

6 I _____ buy that CD but I'm not sure. (can/may)

3 **Read and make sentences. Use the verbs in brackets.**

1 Your friend starts to feel ill in class. What's your advice to him?
   (ought to) _____

2 Your friend isn't wearing his school uniform. What do you say to him?
   (shouldn't) _____

3 You and your friend never arrive in class on time. What do you suggest?
   (ought not) _____

4 You never remember to take your sports kit to school. What do you say to yourself?
   (mustn't) _____

*Remember! **should** and **ought to** have the same meaning.*

4 **Complete the sentences with the verbs in the box.**

| get rid of   get away   get on with   get over   get out of |

1 Sally can't _____ her disappointment at failing her exams.

2 I don't want to go to the party but I don't know how to _____ it.

3 We need to _____ these old clothes.

4 Everyone likes Paul. He's very easy to _____.

5 We tied a rope round the horse's neck so that it couldn't _____.

Individual writing: writing about your opinion

You have read about Julie Smith's **opinion** of zoos. What do you think about homework? You are going to make notes and write your **opinion** of homework.

Read Student's Book page 84 again. It tells you how to write about your opinion.

Choose whether you think homework is a good thing or a bad thing.

My opinion: I think homework is a _____ thing.

Make notes on three reasons to support your opinion.

Reason 1 _____
_____

Reason 2 _____
_____

Reason 3 _____
_____

Write about your opinion.

Homework is a _____ thing

I think homework is a _____ thing for these reasons.

My first reason is _____
_____
_____
_____
_____

My second reason is _____
_____
_____
_____

Another reason why I think homework is a _____ thing is that _____
_____
_____
_____

Listening and speaking

1 Complete the dialogue. Use the words and expressions from the boxes.

| ought to   Might   shouldn't   maybe |
| modern   traditional   skyscrapers |
| library   architect   storeys |
| views   location   design   floor |

| You've got to be joking!   my kind of thing |
| I'm not sure   in my opinion   deadly serious |
| To be honest   Certainly not!   I agree |

Holly: What do you think about the new _____, Ross?
Ross: Well, I like the _____ because I like _____ buildings but _____ they _____ build it in the park.
Holly: _____. The _____ is all wrong.
Ross: Do you like the design?
Holly: _____, it's not _____. I prefer _____ buildings.
Ross: I love _____ – the taller the better. We _____ have one in Hampton.
Holly: How many _____?
Ross: _____. Twenty? Thirty?
Holly: _____!
Ross: No, I'm _____. Wouldn't you like to see one?
Holly: _____! I'd hate it.
Ross: Imagine the _____ from the top _____!
Holly: _____ you become an _____ one day?
Ross: Yes, _____. I'd like that.

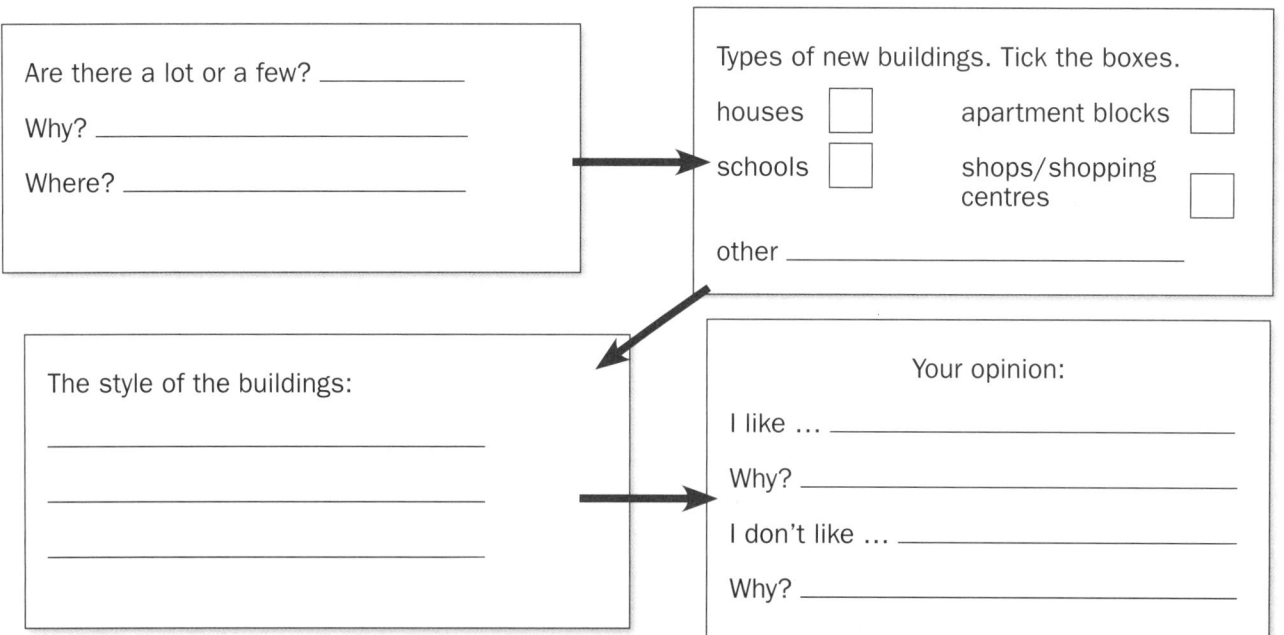

Individual speaking

1 You are going to talk about new buildings in your town. Make notes.

Are there a lot or a few? _____
Why? _____
Where? _____

Types of new buildings. Tick the boxes.
houses ☐   apartment blocks ☐
schools ☐   shops/shopping centres ☐
other _____

The style of the buildings:
_____
_____

Your opinion:
I like … _____
Why? _____
I don't like … _____
Why? _____

2 Write sentences about new buildings in your town. Make notes.

3 Talk about new buildings in your town.

Check-out 8

Reading

1 You read a blog. a What was the writer against? _____   b How many people had posted responses? _____
2 Which of these were on the web page?

   photos   map   caption   advertisement   membership offer   questionnaire   quiz   related links

Vocabulary

1 You learned 20 words to do with animals in captivity. Look at page 124 in this book.
   Do you know what all these words mean? Check any that you are not sure of in your dictionary.
2 Write the negative prefix *in-* or *im-* before these words.

   a _____credible   b _____possible   c _____perfect   d _____visible   e _____direct   f _____patient

3 Write a homophone for each of these words.

   a sure _____   b mail _____   c allowed _____   d floe _____

4 Complete the words with *ci* or *ti*:

   a pre___ ___ous   b pa___ ___ent   c cau___ ___ous   d an___ ___ent

Grammar

1 Complete the sentences. Use the verbs in brackets; use the correct modal.

   a If you _____ (be) interested in animals, you _____ (enjoy) this nature programme.
   b The students _____ (see) the king's crown if they _____ (visit) the museum.
   c The sky is dark and I think it _____ (rain). Perhaps we _____ (go) indoors.
   d This is a new dress and I _____ (get wet) or mum will be cross.

2 Underline the correct phrase. The king could not *get over / get rid of / get out of* the death of his son.

Writing

1 Complete these features of expressing a point of view.

   In the first _____ you must say what you are writing about. In the following paragraphs you write your
   r_____ for your view. When you give your o_____, you write in the _____
   person.

2 Have you made a neat copy of your view about homework? ☐   Is it in your folder? ☐

Listening and speaking

1 Have you listened again to Holly and Ross talking about buildings? ☐
2 Have you and your friend discussed the building in the photographs? ☐
3 Have you listened to Maggie James and understood her speech? ☐
4 Have you talked for one minute about new buildings in your town / city? ☐

Check-out 8 complete ☐

Revision 4 (Units 7 and 8)

1 Complete the sentences with the verbs in the box. Be sure to use the correct forms of the verbs.

go   rise   continue   do   melt   see   keep   drop   protest   use   freeze   suffer

1 If the temperature _____ below zero, water _____.
2 Ice _____ if the temperature _____ above zero.
3 Our bodies always _____ energy if we _____ physical work.
4 You _____ animals in captivity if you _____ to the zoo tomorrow.
5 If they _____ this lion in a cage, it _____ from stress.
6 Unless we _____ against animal cruelty, it _____.

2 Rewrite the sentences. Use *unless*.

1 If we do not protect the Arctic, polar bears will become extinct.
_____

2 Many animals will disappear if we do not protect them.
_____

3 Complete the sentences with one of the words or phrases in brackets.

1 How _____ escalators are there in the shopping centre? (much / many)
2 There are _____ shoppers here this morning. (a lot of / a little)
3 I can see _____ people in the café. (a little / a few)
4 There's _____ jewellery in that window display. (lots of / many)
5 I can't see _____ cheap necklaces or bracelets. (some / any)
6 I've only got _____ money. (a little / a few)
7 There's too _____ noise in here. (much / many)
8 Who should we interview? _____ ideas? (Some / Any)

4 Complete the sentences with one of the verbs in brackets.

1 If you are thirsty, you _____ drink some water. (should / mustn't)
2 Look at those dark clouds. There _____ be a storm later. (ought to / might)
3 You _____ always speak politely to your teachers. (may / must)
4 _____ I borrow your dictionary, please? (Should / Can)
5 Anna _____ decide to study medicine but she's not sure. (may / must)
6 If Freddie wants to be on the team, he _____ train harder. (may / ought to)

5 Complete the sentences with words from the box. Make any necessary changes.

| sauce | stress | prepare | convinced | fridge | ingredients |
| cruel | behaviour | ban | fresh | captivity | fry |

1 When you are cooking, it is always best to use _____ _____.
2 When you _____ the burgers, put the meat in the _____ until you are ready to start cooking.
3 _____ the burgers in a little olive oil. Serve them with tomato _____.
4 Julie believes that keeping animals in _____ is _____.
5 Many animals in zoos suffer from _____ and their _____ is not natural.
6 Julie is _____ that zoos should be _____.

6 Write the past participles of these verbs.

1 break _____   2 steal _____   3 fall _____
4 beat _____   5 chop _____   6 polish _____

7 Use the past participles in Exercise 6 as adjectives in these sentences.

1 Add salt and pepper to the _____ eggs.
2 We used the _____ trees to make a raft.
3 Joe looked very smart in a dark suit and _____ shoes.
4 Mr Duffy mended the _____ chair.
5 Mix some _____ herbs with the meat.
6 The police never found the _____ pictures.

8 Make the opposites by adding *in-*, *im-* or *un-* to these adjectives.

1 ____polite   2 ____important   3 ____visible   4 ____intelligent
5 ____credible   6 ____patient   7 ____correct   8 ____possible

9 Complete the sentences with the words in the box.

| rid of | over | on with | up | down | into |

1 Jenny was invited on a trip to Paris but she turned the invitation _____.
2 It was a cold, wet day but a huge crowd turned _____ to watch the match.
3 To get _____ the mice in his barn, the farmer bought a cat.
4 Billy is easy to talk to. He gets _____ everybody.
5 Susie was very lazy at first but she has turned _____ an excellent student.
6 Fred's illness was serious. It took him months to get _____ it completely.

Revision 4 (Units 7 and 8)

9 How the body works

Reading comprehension

1 Read *How we see* again.

2 Number the sentences in the correct order. The diagram may help you.

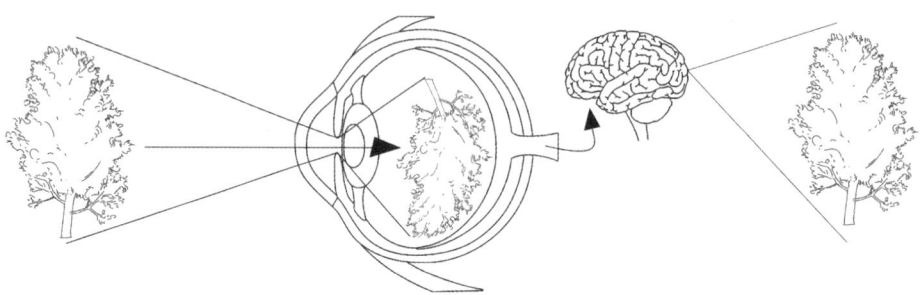

a ____ The lens focuses light onto the retina.

b ____ The brain receives the message and turns the picture the right way round.

c ____ The iris controls the amount of light that enters the eye.

d ____ The optic nerve sends the electrical message from the retina to the brain.

e ____ It turns the picture into an electrical message for the brain.

f ____ The retina shows the picture you are seeing upside-down.

g ____ The pupil becomes bigger in dull light and smaller in bright light.

h ____ Next, the light passes through the lens.

i ____ First, light passes into your eye through the pupil.

j ____ It makes the pupil larger or smaller.

3 Read and complete the sentences. Use the words in the box.
Use the pictures to help you with ideas for filling some of the gaps.

| dust | light | hot materials | sharp objects | wind | insects | fast-moving object |

1 People who go _____ or climb mountains often wear _____ to protect their eyes from the sun reflecting on the snow, which creates very bright and harmful _____.

2 People who work with _____ need good eye protection such as a _____ made of _____. This can also prevent _____ from entering the eye.

3 Motorbike riders wear _____ to protect their eyes from _____, from _____ flying in the air and _____ blowing up from the road.

4 Baseball players are in danger of being hit by a _____ – the baseball. They need very strong protection and their _____ are made of _____.

76 Unit 9 Reading comprehension: sentence order; cloze

Vocabulary

1 Circle the words that are parts of the eye.

| lens | iris | brain | cornea | camera | retina | optic nerve |
| muscle | pupil | vision | visor | sclera | movie |

2 Label the diagram with words from Exercise 1. Use the words to complete the explanation.

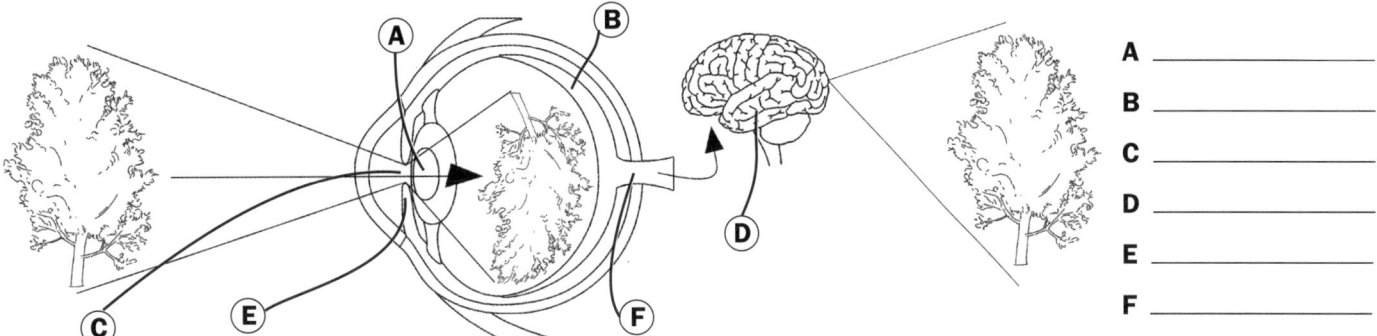

A _____
B _____
C _____
D _____
E _____
F _____

1 Light passes through the _____ which is the hole at the front of the eye.

2 The size of the pupil is controlled by the _____ which is the coloured part of the eye.

3 Light passes through the _____ which changes shape to make the picture as clear as possible.

4 The _____ shows the picture you are seeing upside-down.

5 The _____ sends an electrical message.

6 The electrical message reaches the _____ which turns the picture the right way up.

3 This picture shows the human eye as we are used to seeing it. Label the parts.

| eyelid | eyebrow | eyelash | tear | pupil | iris |

4 Check you understand the meanings of these words. Write them in the correct lists.

| upper | approximately | transparent | automatically | tough | human |

adverbs _____

adjectives _____

Which word can be used as both a noun and an adjective? _____

Unit 9 Vocabulary: cloze; labelling; word classes

Working with words

1 **Rewrite these words to make adjectives ending -ible or -able.**

1 horr_____   2 comfort_____   3 sense_____
4 like_____   5 vis_____   6 terr_____

Be careful of verbs ending -e.

2 **Write the opposite of these words. Use in-, im- or un-.**
Check in your dictionary if you are not sure.

1 credible _____   2 visible _____   3 possible _____   4 divisible _____

5 breakable _____   6 separable _____   7 loveable _____   8 believable _____

3 **Choose the best word from Exercises 1 and 2 to complete these sentences. Use each word once only.**

1 I thought that film was _____. The story was ridiculous and completely _____.
2 This glass is _____. If you drop it on the floor it won't even crack.
3 Thirty-six is _____ by three and four. It is _____ by five.
4 The special effects in the film were _____! The creatures from space were really _____ – they had four eyes and horns on their heads.
5 These shoes are very _____. Is it _____ to change them?
6 Ben is a very _____ boy. He works hard and he has lots of _____ ideas.

4 **Complete the sentences with the verb and the gerund. Circle the gerund.**

1 Ben likes _____. He's _____ a horse at the moment.
2 Anna is _____ her trumpet. She enjoys _____ it.
3 Grandma is _____ a letter. I think _____ letters is difficult.
4 Ned is good at _____. He is _____ in the marathon next month.

5 **abc Spelling: complete the nouns. Write them next to the correct verb below.**

a explo_____   b inclu_____   c deci_____   d revi_____

1 revise _____   2 decide _____   3 explode _____   4 include _____

6 **abc Write the correct ending to these words.**
Use -sion, -ssion, -tion or -shion.

1 sta____   2 fa____   3 mi____   4 vi____   5 cu____
6 na____   7 confu____   8 discu____   9 impre____

Grammar

1 Complete the sentences with the verbs in brackets. Use the passive. Be careful to use the correct tense.

1. A valuable painting _____ from the museum last night. (steal)
2. I hope that the thief _____ soon. (catch)
3. What's happened to the house? All the windows _____. (break)
4. Our eyes _____ by eyelids and eyelashes. (protect)
5. Snow goggles _____ first _____ by the Inuit people. (wear)
6. This scarf is soft and warm because it _____ of silk. (make)
7. Next year a new library _____ in the centre of town. (build)
8. Something is missing from the square. The statue _____ away. (take)

2 Rewrite the sentences. Use the passive.

1. Someone has eaten all the chocolates.   *All the chocolates* _____
2. Someone left the gates open. _____
3. They paint their house every year. _____
4. We will send a reply immediately. _____
5. People grew rice in this valley. _____
6. Someone has swept the floor. _____

3 Answer the questions. Use the passive and the phrases in the box.

> a Russian author   customers in the Middle East   heavy rain
> an unknown artist   an Italian architect

1. Who will design the building?
   The building _____
2. Who drew the pictures?
   _____
3. Who wrote this book?
   _____
4. What has damaged the crops?
   _____
5. Who buys this expensive jewellery?
   _____

Grammar in use

1 Match the sentences with the correct question tags. Write the letters.

1 The market is busy, _____
2 Loads of people come here, _____
3 The crockery isn't expensive, _____
4 You don't like shopping, _____
5 The stalls are colourful, _____
6 We aren't in a hurry, _____
7 They don't sell cutlery, _____
8 The honey tastes good, _____

A is it?
B are we?
C isn't it?
D do you?
E do they?
F aren't they?
G doesn't it?
H don't they?

2 Write the question tags.

Don't forget the question marks!

1 The market is popular, _____
2 You don't like it, _____
3 She's selling honey, _____
4 Markets are cheap, _____
5 That man doesn't look well, _____
6 Lemons taste sour, _____
7 This pan costs a lot, _____
8 We don't have much time, _____

3 Look at the picture and write sentences with question tags. Use your own ideas. Use the question tags in the box.

| isn't it?   aren't they?   doesn't it?   are they?   do they? |

1 _____
2 _____
3 _____
4 _____
5 _____

4 Complete the sentences with the verbs in the box.

| shut out   shut down   shut up   shut off   shut in |

1 The workmen should _____ the electricity before they touch the cables.
2 Annie _____ herself _____ the bathroom and refused to come out.
3 The boy covered his ears with his hands to _____ the noise of the storm.
4 When the factory _____, one hundred people lost their jobs.
5 My sisters chatter all the time. They never _____.

80 Unit 9 Grammar in use: question tags; Grammar extra: phrasal verbs with *shut*

Individual writing: writing an explanation

You have read an **explanation** of how the eye works. You have written an **explanation** of how the lungs work. Now you are going to write an **explanation** to show how you get ready for school and how you travel to school each morning.

Read Student's Book page 94 again. It shows you how to write an **explanation**.

Here are some things to think about. Make notes:

- What time do you get up?

- What do you do as soon as you get up?
    - have breakfast?
    - get washed and dressed?

- What do you have for breakfast?

- When do you pack your school bag?

- What do you put in it?

- Do you take something to eat?

- What do you take?

- When do you get it ready?

- What is the last thing you do before leaving the house?

- What time do you leave the house?

- How do you travel to school?

- What time do you arrive?

Here are some *sentence beginnings* that will be useful.

| First ... | Next ... | As soon as ... | After that ... |
| When I finish ... | At _____ o'clock | | Before I ... |

Write your explanation. Write it in the order you do things in the morning.

Unit 9 Planning sheet for writing an explanation 81

Listening and speaking

Complete the dialogue. Use the words and expressions from the boxes.

do you	doesn't she	don't they	isn't it
aren't they	stall	prices	free sample
delicious	colourful	greedy	popular

loads of stuff	over there	Honestly!
Don't be mean!	Gosh!	Good idea
Here we are!	Not really	I suppose so
Let's have a look

Laura: _____! Goose Lane Market.
Ross: _____! It's busy, _____?
Laura: Yes, it's very _____. You can buy _____ here.
Ross: _____ at some of the stalls.
Laura: Right. How about that fruit and vegetable _____? It's so _____! I'll take a photo.
Ross: Those strawberries look _____, _____?
Laura: Yes, they do.
Ross: Do you think the stallholder will give me a _____?
Laura: _____! You're so _____!
Ross: _____! I just like my food.
Laura: The _____ are really low here, _____?
Ross: _____.
Laura: You don't know much about shopping, _____?
Ross: _____. But I'm good at interviews.
Laura: Why don't you interview that lady _____?
Ross: _____. She looks friendly, _____?

Individual speaking

You are going to talk about a market in your town or a market you have visited. Read the questions and make notes.

Where is it? _____ When does it open? _____

What can you buy there? Circle the items.

Anything else? _____

Circle the words which describe the market.

busy   noisy   quiet   popular   cheap   expensive   interesting

When did you go there? _____ What did you buy? _____

Did you like it? _____ Will you go there again? _____

2 Write sentences about the market.   **3** Talk about the market.

Check-out 9

Reading

1 You read an explanation of part of your body.

   a What part was it? _____   b What passes into it? _____   c What turns the image the right way up? _____

2 Write the things that people wear to protect their eyes from

   a sunlight _____   b hot sparks _____   c wind and dust _____

Vocabulary

1 You learned 20 words about the eye and sight. Look at page 124 in this book.
   Do you know what all these words mean? Check any that you are not sure of in your dictionary.

2 Complete these words using -ible or -able.

   a terr____   b break____   c believ____   d sens____   e divis____   f lov____

3 Use the gerund to complete the sentence.

   I go to the pool to swim every day. _____ in the pool is good exercise.

4 Complete these words with -sion or -ssion:

   a televi____   b discu____   c impre____   d vi____   e mi____   f se____   g confu____

Grammar

1 Complete the sentences using the passive form.

   This museum _____ (build) a year ago. It _____ (not open) yet because it _____ (not finish). It _____ (finish) next month.

2 Write the correct question tag.

   a This programme is hilarious, _____? The characters are a bit weird, though, _____?

   b You don't want to turn over, _____? Yes, but I think Ben wants to watch it, _____?

3 Underline the correct phrase. Mum lost her door key so we were *shut off / shut out / shut down* when we got home.

Writing

1 Complete these features of an explanation.

   An explanation is written in the _____ tense. It uses the present _____ and the present _____. The explanation includes _____ which help to show how things work.

2 Have you made a neat copy of your explanation? ☐   Is it in your folder? ☐

Listening and speaking

1 Have you listened again to Laura and Ross talking about the market? ☐

2 Have you and your friend talked about a market in your town? ☐

3 Did you listen to Laura's interview with the stall holder and answer the questions? ☐

4 Have you told the class about a market you have visited? ☐

Check-out 9 complete ☐

10 Later that day...

Reading comprehension

1 Read *A helping hand* again.

2 Answer these questions. Use short answers.

1. Where was Grandma at the start of the story? _____
2. Where did Mum go the next evening? _____
3. What subject was Sadie studying? _____
4. What was Dad's idea for cheering up Grandma? _____
5. What did Annette need to concentrate on? _____
6. Where did Mum buy the material for the new curtains? _____
7. What did Annette make for Grandma? _____
8. What did Annette receive as her prize? _____
9. What did Annette decide to study the next year? _____
10. What did Grandma give Annette? _____

3 Number these sentences in the order of the events in the story.

a _____ Grandma went to see the medical faculty at the university.
b _____ Annette just laughed.
c _____ Mum breathed another sigh of relief.
d _____ Sadie got her exam results.
e _____ Grandma saw the picture of Sadie and her friends beaming in front of the lemon tree.
f __1__ Grandma was in hospital.
g _____ Mum chose new curtain material for Grandma's room.
h _____ Mum was relieved when she heard about Grandma's successful operation.
i _____ Annette gave Grandma an album of photographs.
j _____ Annette entered the competition.
k _____ Everyone was pleased and impressed.
l _____ Everyone thought of ideas to cheer up Grandma.
m _____ Annette received an envelope.
n _____ Mum was concerned because Grandma was feeling lonely.

Vocabulary

1 Write the verbs next to the correct definition. Do as many as you can without looking in your dictionary. Use your dictionary to check answers and complete the exercise.

| embarrass | miss | pause | come round |
| suggest | enquire | regain | inspire | glance | concentrate |

1. to stop an action for a while before continuing it _____
2. to make someone feel silly in front of other people _____
3. to visit someone in their home _____
4. to think about something with complete attention _____
5. to ask _____
6. to encourage someone to do something by giving exciting ideas about it _____
7. to look quickly _____
8. to have again _____
9. to put forward an idea _____
10. to feel sad because something or someone is not present _____

2 Complete the sentences with the adverbs in the box.

| modestly | ultimately | cheerfully | eventually | enquiringly |

1. "We haven't got that computer at the moment but could I order it for you?" said the shop assistant _____.
2. "Hurray! I've learned all the irregular verbs," said Ben _____.
3. Ben was proud to win the prize but he accepted it _____ and thanked his teacher.
4. Dad tried to mend our car but _____ he had to agree it was hopeless.
5. We walked for hours and _____ we reached the lake before we went through the forest.

3 Check you understand the meanings of these nouns. Write them in the correct lists.

| cheerfulness | opera | opportunity | album | certainty | chemistry | gallery | talent |

common nouns _____ _____ _____ _____
abstract nouns _____ _____ _____ _____

4 Write the adjectives in alphabetical order. Check you understand the meanings.

radiant   shimmering   translucent   concerned   depressed   crisp   tremendous   biological

_____

5 Choose four adjectives from Exercise 4 and use them in sentences of your own.

_____
_____
_____
_____

Working with words

1 Rewrite these sentences as two separate sentences.

1 The nurses stood on the hospital steps, waving goodbye to Grandma.
   _____
   _____

2 Annette arranged the photos in the album, singing quietly to herself.
   _____
   _____

3 Dad, glancing quickly behind him, took the last chocolate out of the box.
   _____
   _____

2 Rewrite these pairs of sentences to make one sentence. Use an extra clause.

1 Grandma sat in the car. She waved goodbye to the nurses.
   _____

2 The children were laughing and shouting. They ran into the playground.
   _____

3 The lemon tree had bright yellow fruit on its branches. It stood on the balcony.
   _____

3 Complete these words. Use your dictionary to help you if you need it.

1 t__ __m__nd__ __s   very good, excellent

2 h__ __re__d__u__   terrible, awful

3 __n__ __mo__ __   very large

4 obv__ __us   clear, evident

5 ca__t__o__s   slow and careful

6 vic__ __ __s   very nasty and cruel

4 abc Spelling: complete the words using -er or -re.

1 entertain__ __   2 theat__ __   3 lit__ __   4 lett__ __   5 ent__ __
6 cent__ __   7 rubb__ __   8 fib__ __   9 somb__ __

5 abc Find the words in Exercise 4 that match these definitions.

1 a measurement for liquid _____   2 the middle point _____

3 a thread of material _____   4 dull and gloomy _____

Grammar

1 Complete the sentences with the verbs in the box.
Use the present perfect simple.

| drink | take | hurt |
| wear | begin | spent |

1 Ouch! I _____ my toe!
2 Annette _____ not _____ her English project yet.
3 How many photos _____ you _____?
4 Someone _____ all the milk. The bottle is empty.
5 We _____ always _____ our holidays at the seaside.
6 Billy _____ glasses since he was seven.

2 Look at the pictures. Write what they have been doing and for how long.
Use the present perfect continuous and *since* or *for*.

1 an hour   <u>They have been playing football for an hour.</u>

2 early this morning _____

3 four o'clock _____

4 two weeks _____

5 ten minutes _____

6 1996 _____

3 Answer the questions about yourself.

1 How long have you been at your school? _____
2 How long have you lived in your town? _____
3 What is the weather like today? _____
4 How long has it been like this? _____
5 What have you been doing today? _____
6 How many years have you been studying English? _____

Grammar in use

1 Complete the sentences with the verbs in the box. Use the present perfect.

| win | take | ride | enter | see | eat |

1. Laura _____ never _____ Morris dancing.
2. Ross _____ never _____ a pony before.
3. _____ you ever _____ a prize?
4. _____ Jack ever _____ a fancy dress competition?
5. _____ we ever _____ a more delicious cake?
6. I _____ never _____ a photo with this camera.

2 Complete the sentences with the verbs in brackets. Use the present perfect or the past simple.

1. We _____ our holidays in the mountains last year. (spend)
2. _____ you ever _____ this song before? (hear)
3. _____ you _____ cakes at the Town Fair yesterday? (buy)
4. Holly _____ never _____ to Goose Lane Market. (be)
5. A lot of snow _____ last night. (fall)
6. So much snow _____ never _____ before. (fall)

3 Complete the dialogue. Use the present perfect and the past simple of the verbs in brackets.

(be, go, see)

Billy: _____ you ever _____ to Australia?

Fred: Yes, I have.

Billy: When _____ you _____ there?

Fred: I _____ there last summer.

Billy: _____ you _____ any kangaroos?

Fred: Yes, we _____ lots of them.

Billy: Lucky you! I _____ never _____ a kangaroo.

4 Complete the sentences with the phrasal verbs in the box.

| go on | go by | go over | go into | go off |

1. We _____ all the details of our journey very carefully before we left.
2. Jessie doesn't eat meat any more. She says she has _____ it.
3. Dan is a talented fiddle player. He should _____ practising.
4. Katy loves children so she has decided to _____ teaching.
5. We were having such fun that the time _____ really quickly.

Unit 10 Grammar in use: present perfect with *ever* / *never*; present perfect and past simple; Grammar extra: phrasal verbs with *go*

Individual writing: writing a story with a simple plot

10

In Unit 6, you read about George. He visited Mr Duffy to collect a present for his cousin, Sally. It was a small blue and white boat with three wooden sailors. Now you are going to write **what happens next**.

Read Student's Book page 104 again. It shows you how to write a **story** with a simple plot.

Write a story with this plot:

| What part of the story? | How do you know time has passed? | What happens? |

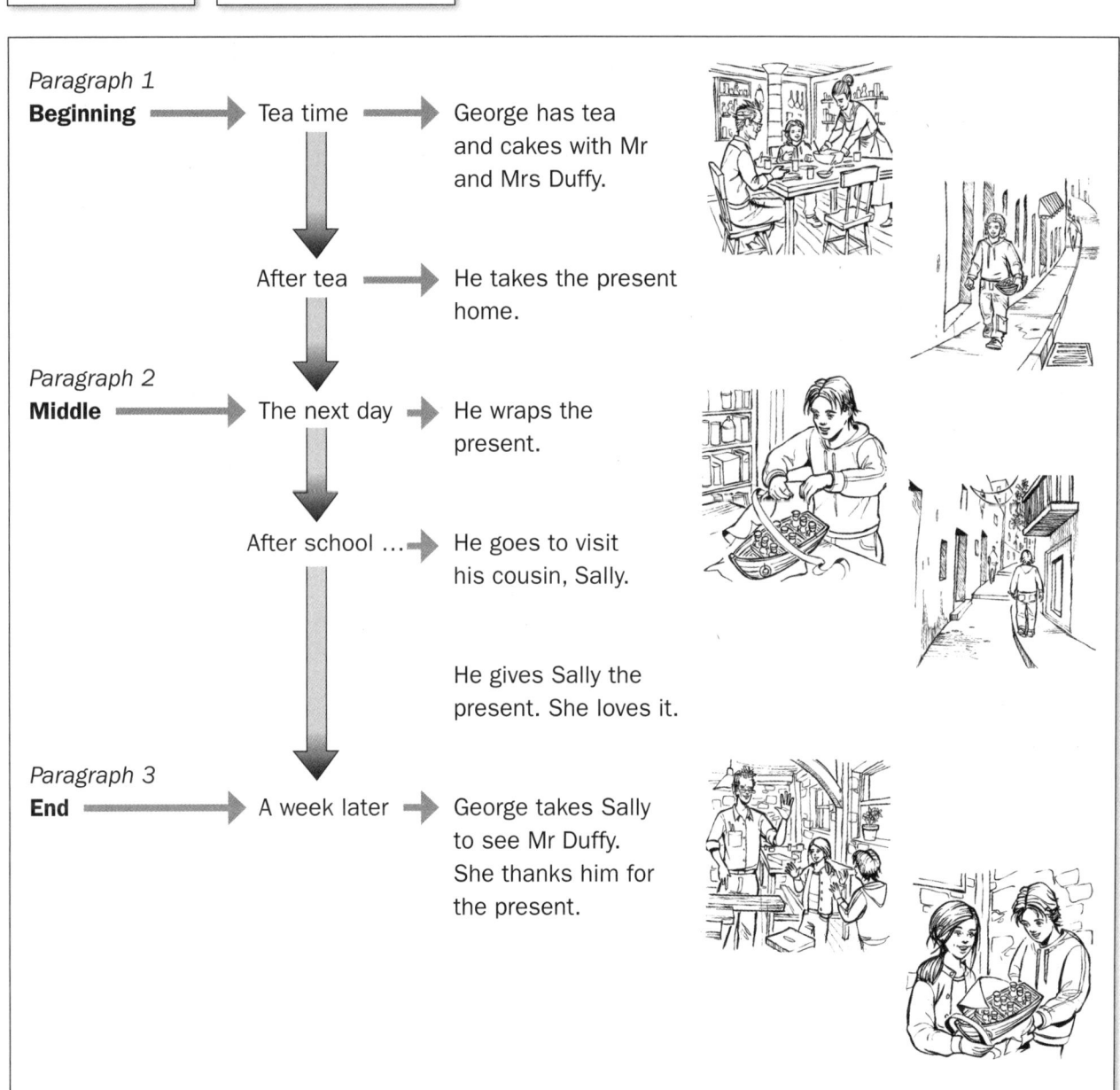

Paragraph 1 **Beginning** → Tea time → George has tea and cakes with Mr and Mrs Duffy.

After tea → He takes the present home.

Paragraph 2 **Middle** → The next day → He wraps the present.

After school ... → He goes to visit his cousin, Sally.

He gives Sally the present. She loves it.

Paragraph 3 **End** → A week later → George takes Sally to see Mr Duffy. She thanks him for the present.

Unit 10 Planning sheet for writing a story with a simple plot

Listening and speaking

1 Complete the dialogue. Use the words and expressions from the boxes.

taken	been	found	carrying	see	went	What on earth	Honestly!	I mean
is it	aren't they	Have you	wasn't	never	ago	Let's have a look!	It's awesome!
Chinese	magazine	new year	dragons			I think	actually	I get it!

Laura: I've _____ a great picture in this _____.
Ross: _____! Oh!
Laura: They're _____ dancers! They're great, _____?
Ross: _____ are they doing?
Laura: They're _____ a dragon on their heads.
Ross: Why?
Laura: Because they're celebrating the Chinese _____.
Ross: Oh, _____! It isn't a real dragon, _____?
Laura: No, silly! _____! You're hopeless!
Ross: Where was this photo _____? _____!
Laura: In Hong Kong, _____.
Ross: Have you ever _____ there? To Hong Kong, _____.
Laura: No, _____. Why? _____?
Ross: I have, _____. I _____ there two years _____.
But it _____ new year so I didn't _____ any _____.

Individual speaking

1 You are going to talk about a festival you have been to or a festival that you know about. Make notes.

Name of the festival: _____
What are the people celebrating? _____
Location: _____
When does it take place? _____

What is special about the festival? Tick (✔).
A parade ☐   Costumes ☐
Music ☐   Dancing ☐
Food and drink ☐   Anything else? ☐
Give details: _____
_____

When did you go to this festival? _____
What did you like about it? _____
What didn't you like about it? _____

OR

Would you like to go to this festival? _____
Why?/Why not? _____

2 Write sentences.

3 Talk about the festival.

Check-out 10

Reading

1. You read a narrative story with a clear plot.

   a When the story began, where was Grandma? _____

   b Who was worried? _____   c Who was lonely? _____

2. a Later, who passed her exams? _____   b Who made a book of photographs? _____

3. a At the end of the story, who was relieved? _____

   b Who felt confident? _____   c Who was cheerful? _____

Vocabulary

1. You learned 20 words to do with behaviour and feelings. Look at page 124–5 in this book.
   Do you know what all these words mean? Check any that you are not sure of in your dictionary.

2. Underline the clause in this sentence which gives extra information about the subject.

   The children ran across the playground, laughing and shouting as they went.

3. Write the adjectives from these nouns.

   a nerve _____   b marvel _____   c fury _____   d ridicule _____   e courage _____

4. Complete these words with -re or -er.   a met____   b cent____   c mutt____   d theat____

Grammar

1. Complete the sentences with the correct form of the verb in brackets and *since* or *for*.

   How long have the children been playing? Ben and Jack _____ (throw) stones in the lake _____ ten minutes. Sue and Andy _____ (ride) their bikes _____ two o'clock.

2. Complete the sentences with the present perfect or the past simple.

   Ben: _____ you ever _____ (swim) a kilometre? Last summer we _____ (stay) at the seaside and I _____ (learn) to swim.

   Jack: Lucky you. I _____ never _____ (see) the sea.

3. Underline the correct phrase. Always *go into / go over / go by* your work before you hand it in.

Writing

1. Complete these features of a narrative story. The plot has a clear b_____, m_____ and e_____.

2. Time phrases show passing time. Underline the phrases that tell you that time has passed.

   the following morning   at ten o'clock   later that week   the next day   tomorrow afternoon

3. Have you made a neat copy of your narrative story? ☐   Is it in your folder? ☐

Listening and speaking

1. Have you listened again to Holly and Jack talking about international festivals? ☐

2. Have you talked for one minute about a festival you know about? ☐   **Check-out 10 complete** ☐

Revision 5 (Units 9 and 10)

1 **Complete the sentences with the verbs in brackets. Use the passive. Be careful to use the correct tense.**

1 Last night trees _____ over by a violent storm. (blow)

2 Next year a new shopping centre _____ outside the town. (build)

3 Look at this beautiful old dress! It _____ never _____. (wear)

4 Fruit and vegetables _____ in the market square every Monday. (sell)

2 **Change the sentences. Use the passive. Use *by* in three sentences.**

1 A young boy wrote these poems. _____

2 Someone has eaten all the cakes. _____

3 The optic nerve sends messages to the brain. _____

4 Every student in the school will take the test. _____

5 People have farmed this land for centuries. _____

3 **Complete the sentences with question tags.**

1 The market's very busy, _____

2 They sell everything here, _____

3 Laura's taking a photo, _____

4 You like honey, _____

5 That stallholder sells cheese, _____

6 The fruit doesn't cost much, _____

7 We aren't late, _____

8 You don't have much time, _____

4 **Complete the sentences with the verbs in brackets. Use the present perfect simple or the present perfect continuous.**

1 Look at all this glass on the floor! Someone _____ the window. (break)

2 Annette is at the park. She _____ photos all morning. (take)

3 _____ the children _____ up yet? (wake)

4 The builders _____ hard all week but they _____ not _____ the house yet. (work, finish)

5 **Complete the sentences with *for* or *since*.**

1 My uncle has lived in Paris _____ three years.

2 Jenny has been learning the violin _____ last September.

3 Mr Martin has worked at our school _____ 2007.

4 We've been waiting for the bus _____ half an hour.

6 **Complete the sentences with the present perfect simple or the past simple. Use the verbs in the box.**

| write   eat   go   see   be |

1 I _____ to America last summer. _____ you ever _____ to America?

2 My brother _____ a bear in the forest but I _____ never _____ one.

3 We _____ never _____ Japanese food but we _____ some Chinese food last weekend.
4 _____ you _____ your composition yet? I _____ mine last night.

7 Complete the sentences with the words in the box. Make any necessary changes.

vision   human   brain   tough   muscle   approximately

1 _____ have better _____ than many other mammals. We can see _____ ten million different shades of colour.
2 Our _____ controls the _____ in our bodies.
3 Some fruits have _____ skins, which are impossible to eat.

8 Write the words in the box next to their definitions.

pause   glance   talent   eventually   concerned
enquire   regain   depressed   opportunity

1 worried adj _____
2 look quickly v _____
3 chance n _____
4 in the end adv _____
5 great skill n _____
6 sad adj _____
7 get back v _____
8 stop for a short time v _____
9 ask v _____

9 Make adjectives by adding -ible, -able or -ous.

1 vis_____   2 nerv_____   3 lov_____   4 courage_____
5 believ_____   6 sens_____   7 ridicul_____   8 terr_____

10 Complete the sentences with adjectives from Exercise 9.

1 This film is stupid. In fact, it's completely _____.
2 What a _____ kitten! It's so sweet!
3 There was a _____ storm last night.
4 Susie felt very _____ before her exam.
5 The fog was so thick that no lights were _____.
6 The girl's story was sad but completely _____.

11 Complete the sentences with the words in the box.

off   over   up   out   down   on

1 I put my hands over my ears to shut _____ the noise.
2 Jane used to like the colour pink but now she's gone _____ it.
3 The factory shut _____ because it was not successful.
4 My little brother is always talking. He refuses to shut _____.
5 I asked him to be quiet but he went _____ talking.
6 James went _____ all the irregular verbs before his test.

Revision 5 (Units 9 and 10)

11 Sports reports

Reading comprehension

1 Read *A match with a difference* again.

2 Answer these questions. Use short answers.

1. Who wrote this article? _____
2. What competition was being played and what was the score? _____
3. How many spectators were there? _____
4. What was unexpected about the semi-final? _____
5. What did most people think the hot-air balloon was at first? _____
6. Which two people commented on Mr Flynn's arrival? _____
7. What change did Mr Flynn tell the spectators about? _____
8. How quickly did City take the lead? _____
9. What event happened at half-time? _____
10. Which player was substituted after 35 minutes? _____

3 Complete the sentences with the words in the box.

| relax | address | equalise | descend | soar | sink |

1. The green and yellow hot-air balloon _____ over the stadium.
2. Gradually it _____ lower and lower over the stadium.
3. Finally it _____ to the centre of the pitch.
4. After the hot-air balloon had landed, Fergal Flynn _____ the crowd.
5. The City players could not _____ for long because United _____.

4 Read the statements. Underline the sentence that best matches the meaning of each one.

1. Da Silva justified his place in the team.
   a. Da Silva showed he could play well in the team.
   b. Da Silva showed that he was worth his place in the team.

2. Jones lost no time in making his mark.
   a. Jones' boot made an impression in the pitch when he scored.
   b. Jones quickly impressed the spectators.

3. The match was full of drama.
   a. The match was thrilling.
   b. The match was well played.

4. Strachan was nowhere near it.
   a. Strachan was close but could not catch it.
   b. Strachan was a long way from it.

Vocabulary

1 Write the words under the correct picture.

cross   pass   foul   tackle   dodge   header   save

1 _____   2 _____   3 _____   4 _____

5 _____   6 _____   7 _____

2 Write the words next to the correct definition.

splendid   jubilant   deliberate   predictable   clumsy   swift   skilful

1 _____ very happy, joyful
2 _____ fast
3 _____ can be expected to happen in a particular way
4 _____ not at all graceful or neat
5 _____ expert, well-done
6 _____ marvellous
7 _____ on purpose

3 Match the adjectives and nouns. Write adjectival phrases. Check back in the article if you need to.

deliberate   spectacular   powerful   clumsy   reserve

striker   tackle   foul   header   save

_____   _____
_____   _____
_____   _____

Unit 11 Vocabulary: football lexis; adjectives, adjectival phrases

Working with words

1 Write the words as compound nouns.

1 skate + board = _____   2 air + port = _____
3 work + bench = _____   4 pen + knife = _____
5 eye + brow = _____   6 beef + burger = _____
7 rail + way = _____   8 brief + case = _____

2 Choose four of the compound nouns and write them in sentences of your own.

_____
_____
_____
_____

3 Explain the meaning of these expressions in your own words.   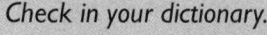 *Check in your dictionary.*

1 never-ending _____
2 well-written _____
3 part-time _____
4 one-way _____
5 mix-up _____
6 man-made _____

4 Complete the sentences with adjectives in Exercise 3.

1 My cousin has a _____ job because he is studying three days a week.
2 Sometimes the rain in England seems to be _____!
3 This story is very _____ and will be in the school magazine.
4 When Ben went home wearing Sam's coat, his mother realised there had been a _____.
5 The Eiffel Tower is a _____ attraction in Paris.
6 You mustn't drive the wrong way down a _____ street.

5 abc Spelling: match the words with the pictures. Use your dictionary to help you if you need to.

| ditch   crutch   stitch   patch   hutch   latch   sketch |

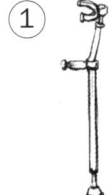   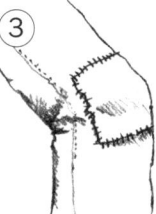  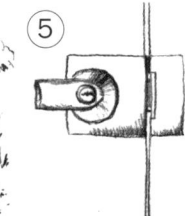 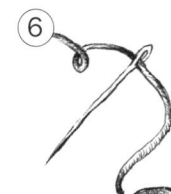 

Grammar

1 Rewrite the sentences as reported speech.

1 "The club's new owner is a clever businessman," said a reporter.
<u>A reporter said that</u> _____

2 "He owns an airline," a man added.
_____

3 "The balloon's landing on the pitch," shouted a fan.
_____

4 "I don't usually travel by balloon," Mr Flynn said.
_____

5 "I'll spend money on new players," he explained.
_____

6 "The club will win the championship," he promised.
_____

7 "We're planning to watch every match," the fans said.
_____

8 "You will like the new club colours," Mr Flynn told the spectators.
_____

Remember! You can say: "He said that ..." or "He said ..."

2 Report what the people say. Use the verbs in brackets.

1 (say, believe, say)

I'm going to a football match. City is a hard team to beat but I think United will win.

_____
_____
_____

2 (tell, say, promise)

Mum! We haven't got any homework. There's a good programme on TV. We'll tidy our rooms afterwards.

_____
_____
_____

Grammar in use

1 **Complete the sentences with *who* or *which*.**

1. A commuter is someone _____ travels to a different town to work every day.
2. The "Park and ride" scheme, _____ started last year, has been very successful.
3. Hampton is a town _____ takes its transport system seriously.
4. Drivers _____ work on the other side of town can use the ring road.
5. The streets _____ are now pedestrian areas used to be very polluted.
6. The cyclists _____ use the cycle lanes now feel much safer.

*Remember! **who** for people, **which** for things.*

2 **Complete the sentences with one of the words in brackets.**

1. We all hate the traffic jams _____ happen during the rush hour. (where / which)
2. There are some streets in town _____ cars are banned. (where / which)
3. People _____ shop in the town centre like the clean, quiet streets. (which / who)
4. Rush hour is the time _____ the streets are the most crowded. (which / when)
5. From here you can catch a bus _____ will take you to the railway station. (who / that)

3 **Rewrite the two sentences to make one sentence. Use the words in brackets.**

1. John missed the train. He was planning to catch it. (which)
   John missed the train which he was planning to catch.

2. We met a man. He was cycling round the world. (who)
   _____

3. Autumn is the season. We get the most storms then. (when)
   _____

4. The bridge has collapsed. It crosses the ring road. (that)
   The bridge that crosses the ring road has collapsed.

5. The car park has been closed. We used to leave our car there. (where)
   _____

6. The pollution has decreased. It was caused by heavy traffic. (which)
   _____

Remember! Sometimes the relative clause is in the middle of the sentence.

4 **Complete the sentences with *make* or *do*.**

1. It's only a spider. Stop _____ such a fuss!
2. Let's go to the shopping centre to _____ our shopping.
3. Joe joined the drama club and immediately _____ his mark with a fine performance in the school play.
4. Some goats got into the garden and _____ a terrible mess.
5. Please _____ the dishes when you have finished eating.

Individual writing: writing a newspaper report

You have read a newspaper **report** about a football match and written about United's match with Rangers in the final. Now you are going to write a newspaper **report** about Fergal Flynn. He likes travelling in his hot-air balloon. After the match against City, he got into his hot-air balloon to go home. The balloon was coming down in his garden when it got caught on a tree. He wasn't hurt but he was stuck in the balloon. Write the newspaper **report**.

Read Student's Book page 114 again. It tells you how to write a **newspaper report**.

Make notes:
What happened?
- Who saw that the hot-air balloon was stuck? _____
- What did they do? _____
- Who came to help? _____
- What did they use to get Fergal down? _____

The facts
- What time was it when the balloon got stuck? _____
- What sort of tree was the balloon stuck in? _____
- How long was Fergal stuck in the balloon? _____

Who said what?
- What did Fergal say when he was on the ground again?

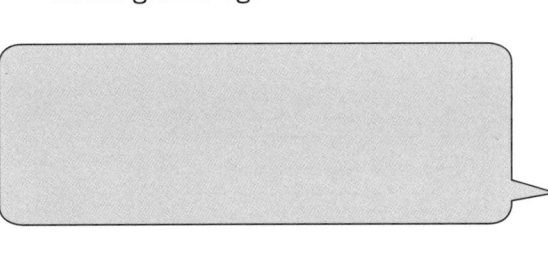

- What did someone who helped say?

Use your notes to write your newspaper report.

Remember!
Think of an interesting headline.

Write your by-line.

Use your opening paragraph to tell the reader what the story is about.

Listening and speaking

1 Complete the dialogue. Use the words and expressions from the boxes.

pass	took	argued	flew	move	travel
by plane	got stuck	boring	sit still	silly
journey	voyage	boats	traffic jam	ages

Me, too	you're right	What a nightmare!
Oh dear	Absolutely!	of course!	you know
Let me see	Honestly!

Holly: How did Ross _____ when he went to New York?
Laura: He _____, of course! _____! You are _____!
Holly: No, I'm not. There are _____ that go to America, _____.
Laura: Yes, _____ but they take _____ to get there.
Holly: How long is the journey _____?
Laura: Hmm ... _____ ... Ross said it _____ six hours, I think.
Holly: Last summer we had a car _____ which was really long. We _____ in a _____ and we didn't _____ one centimetre for two hours.
Laura: Ugh! _____!
Holly: _____! It was so _____ having to _____ all that time.
Laura: How did you _____ the time?
Holly: I _____ with my brother.
Laura: _____ ... One day I'd like to make a long _____ on a beautiful, big ship.
Holly: Mmm ... _____. I'd love it. Without my brother, _____!

Individual speaking

1 Think about a journey you have made by plane, by train or by car.

2 You are going to talk about a journey you made. Make notes.

When? _____   How? _____

From where? _____   To where? _____

Who with? _____   How long? _____

How did you pass the time? _____

Did you enjoy the journey? Why? / Why not? _____

Did anything special / funny / interesting / terrible happen? _____
_____

How did you feel when you arrived at your destination? _____

What did you do when you arrived? _____

3 Write sentences about your journey. Use your notes.

4 Talk about your journey.

Check-out 11

Reading

1. You read a sports report.

   a What was the sport? _____

   b Which teams played? _____

   c What business did the new owner of United have? _____

2. A newspaper sports report usually uses the _____ tense.
   At the beginning of the article there is a short h_____.

Vocabulary

1. You learned 20 words to do with football. Look at page 125 in this book.
   Do you know what all these words mean? Check any that you are not sure of in your dictionary.

2. Write three compound nouns with *sun* as the first word. _____ _____ _____

3. Write three compound nouns with *ball* as the second word. _____ _____ _____

4. Complete this sentence with words ending *-tch*.

   My uncle likes to _____ the football _____ on the _____ in the park.

Grammar

1. Write the reported sentence:

   "This is a brilliant match," said Andy.   _____

2. Answer the question:

   What is a football stadium?   _____

3. Write *make* or *do* to complete the sentences.

   My brother always _____ a fuss when he has to _____ the dishes or _____ the shopping.

Writing

1. Complete these features of a newspaper report.

   The h_____ catches the reader's attention. The opening p_____ must keep readers interested. Usually, events are told in o_____. The report contains f_____. Often there is an exciting p_____ to illustrate the article.

2. Have you made a neat copy of your newspaper story? ☐   Is it in your folder? ☐

Listening and speaking

1. Have you listened again to Laura and Ross talking about travelling? ☐
2. Did your friend ask you where and how you have travelled? ☐
3. Did you ask your friend? ☐
4. Have you talked for one minute about a journey you have made? ☐

Check-out 11 complete ☐

12 On stage

Reading comprehension

1 Read *Danger on the railway* again.

2 Number the sentences in the correct order of the events in the play.

a ___ They waved the flags when they saw the train.

b ___ They put the red cloth on flagpoles.

c ___ Peter told Roberta to keep off the track.

d ___ The children wanted to warn the train.

e ___ They saw a huge landslide on the other side of the valley.

f _1_ The children were going to pick cherries by the railway track.

g ___ The girls took off their red petticoats.

h ___ The landslide completely blocked the track.

i ___ They tore them into pieces.

j ___ Peter said that the 11.29 had not gone by.

3 Who was it? Read the question and write the name.

1 Who heard the weird sound first? _____

2 Who first saw the trees moving? _____

3 Who said it was a landslide? _____

4 Who knew what the time was? _____

5 Who wanted to run to the station? _____

6 Who suggested doing something to the telegraph wires? _____

7 Who thought of waving something red? _____

8 Who thought of the flannel petticoats? _____

9 Who thought of tearing them to make flags? _____

10 Who pushed the flags into the stones in the track? _____

11 Who first heard the train coming? _____

12 Who stood on the track? _____

4 These words tell you how the children felt during the scene.
One word in each line is wrong. Circle the odd one out in each line.

1	thoughtful	puzzled	shocked	scared	amused
2	worried	hot	firm	anxious	furious
3	annoyed	hopeless	excited	desperate	urgent

Vocabulary

1 Read the words and phrases. Check you understand the meanings.

familiar	reach	weird	slip	landslide	shocked	mound	disaster
flannel petticoat		cuckoo	desperately		telegraph post		flagpole
brainwave	accident	top speed	firmly	bush	like mad		urgently

2 Read the words in Exercise 1 again. Write them in the correct lists.

1 two verbs _____ _____

2 three adverbs _____ _____ _____

3 three compound nouns _____ _____ _____

4 three adjectives _____ _____ _____

5 four phrases _____ _____ _____ _____

6 five nouns _____ _____ _____ _____ _____

3 Complete the sentences with the correct word or phrase from Exercise 1.

1 Grandpa met us at the station and we were happy to see his _____ face once again.

2 The bookshelf is too high and I can't _____ the dictionary.

3 Sam's idea for our project was a real _____ and we won the prize.

4 Anna was _____ when she saw the spider in her lunch box.

5 The cat was sleeping in the shade under the _____.

6 When the policeman saw the _____ between the two cars, he picked up his phone and spoke _____.

7 There was a _____ of rocks at the highest point on the mountain.

8 Sometimes, heavy rain falling on a hill or mountain can cause a _____.

9 At the end of the play everyone cheered and clapped _____.

10 We were late for the bus so we ran down the road at _____.

4 Use these words in sentences of your own.

| firmly | disaster | weird | slip | flagpole |

_____

_____

_____

_____

Working with words

1 Decide if each phrase tells you about *time*, *place* or *how* an action is done. Write the correct word after each adverbial phrase.

1 before he opened it _____
2 with a smile _____
3 under the table _____
4 through the door _____
5 after the storm _____
6 in a hurry _____

2 Complete the sentences with the phrases in Exercise 1.

1 Ben looked carefully at the box _____.
2 "How lovely to see you," said Grandma _____.
3 "This is careless homework," said the teacher, "Did you do it _____?"
4 The bag was lying on the floor _____.
5 _____ the road was shiny and wet.
6 The excited children rushed in _____.

3 Complete the sentences with the correct word in the box.

| impressive   protective   active   inventive   attractive |

1 Firefighters wear special _____ clothing.
2 We decorated the table with candles and flowers to make it look _____.
3 Ben is very _____ and he's good at making new things.
4 The teacher liked our project. "It's very _____," he said.
5 Grandad goes swimming every week and he plays chess. He likes to be _____.

4 Look at these adjectives ending *-ive*. Write the words next to the correct definition. Check in your dictionary.

| positive   attentive   secretive |

1 not telling people about things _____
2 certain, sure _____
3 listening to or watching something carefully _____

5 **abc** Spelling: complete the words using *wa-*. Write them in the correct list.

a ___sh   b ___r   c ___rrior   d ___rm   e ___ll   f ___nder

g ___rd   h ___ft   i ___ter   j ___nt

1 sounds like *o* in *spot*   _____ _____ _____ _____ _____
2 sounds like *aw* in *crawl* _____ _____ _____ _____ _____

Unit 12 Working with words: adverbial phrases; suffix *-ive*; Spelling: *a* modified after *w*

Grammar

1 Complete the sentences. Use the verbs in brackets.

*Remember! Past tense in the **if** clause, **would** in the main clause.*

*But you can use **could** in both clauses!*

1 The station is far away. If the station _____ nearer, the children _____ there. (be, run)
2 The train driver does not know about the landslide. If he _____ about the landslide, he _____ stop in time. (know, be able to)
3 The girls are wearing red petticoats. If they _____ off their petticoats, they _____ make red flags. (take, can)
4 Molly hasn't got much money. She _____ some CDs if she _____ more money. (buy, have)
5 It's raining today. If the weather _____ better, we _____ go to the beach. (be, can)
6 Jack is always late for school. He _____ on time if he _____ earlier. (arrive, leave)

2 Read what these people are saying about their town.

There's too much traffic in the town centre. It's very polluted and noisy.

My children want to learn to swim but we don't have a swimming pool in the town.

There's no cinema in the town. We can't go and see new films.

There aren't many good shops. I think we should have a shopping centre.

Write four conditional sentences about their town.
In the first two sentences, put the *if* clause first. In the last two sentences, put the *if* clause second.

1 _____
2 _____
3 _____
4 _____

Unit 12 Grammar: second conditional **105**

Grammar in use

1 Complete the sentences with the correct form of *have to*.

1 Tomorrow we _____ get to school earlier than usual.
2 My uncle _____ take the train to work every day.
3 Last week John's sister _____ go to hospital.
4 You _____ work hard if you want to pass your next exam.
5 Sportsmen _____ eat healthy food.

2 Write questions for these answers.

1 _____
   Yes, the students must wear their uniform to school.
2 _____
   Yes, they have to arrive at school on time.
3 What _____
   They had to buy bread and eggs at the supermarket.
4 When _____
   They must be ready to leave at eight o'clock.
5 How long _____
   He will have to stay at school for another five years.

3 Rewrite these sentences to make them negative.

1 You must speak loudly. _____
2 He has to practise every day. _____
3 They have to walk to school. _____
4 Jane had to revise for the test. _____
5 John will have to stay behind after school. _____
6 Molly had to learn the poem by heart. _____

4 Complete the sentences with the phrasal verbs in the box.

| break off | break into | break down | break up | break out |

1 Last night thieves _____ our school and stole several computers.
2 We're going on holiday the day after we _____ for the summer.
3 Susie _____ a piece of chocolate and put it in her mouth.
4 A serious epidemic has _____ across the whole country.
5 This machine is very old but it has never _____ once.

Individual writing: writing a playscript

You have read a **playscript** from *The Railway Children* about how they saved the train. Now you are going to write a **playscript** for the next scene. Roberta, Phyllis and Peter are waiting at the station to catch the train. The train is late. While they are waiting, they talk about how they saved the other train. Write the **playscript**.

Read Student's Book page 124 again. It tells you how to write a **playscript**.

Make notes:

- the characters _____
  _____
  _____

- the scene _____

- What does Peter say when the train is late? How does he say it?

PETER: (_____) _____

- What does Phyllis say? How does she say it?

PHYLLIS: (_____) _____

- What does Roberta say? How does she say it?

ROBERTA: (_____) _____

- When Peter begins to talk about the other train, what does he say?

PETER: _____

- Roberta doesn't want to talk about the other train. What does she say?

ROBERTA: _____

- The children hear the train arriving.

What do they do? [_____]

What do they say?

PETER: _____
_____

PHYLLIS: _____
_____

ROBERTA: _____
_____

Here are some useful words for stage directions.

angrily	anxiously	calmly	confidently
hurriedly	loudly	politely	
quietly	quickly	slowly	

Use your notes to write your playscript.

Unit 12 Planning sheet for writing a playscript 107

Listening and speaking

1 Complete the dialogue. Use the words and expressions from the boxes.

have to	has to	will have to	had to	must
won	hurts	would be	think
first prize	email	hairdresser's	dentist

Me, too	Guess what?	Shut up!
maybe	I'm not sure	nothing special
anything special	What?	poor you!
How about you

Holly: What are you doing this week, Laura?
Laura: I _____ go to the _____ on Tuesday.
Holly: Oh, _____! I _____ go last week. I hate it.
Laura: _____, but one of my teeth _____ so I really _____ go.
Holly: _____, Jack?
Laura: He _____ go to the _____. His hair is much too long.
Jack: _____! My hair's fine.
Holly: Are you doing _____, Ross?
Ross: No, _____. All I can _____ about is the *Portrait* project.
Laura: The results _____ arrive soon, surely?
Ross: _____. This week _____.
Jack: It _____ amazing if we _____!
Laura: You've got an _____, Ross.
Ross: It's from Professor Brown... Oh! _____?
Holly: _____?
Ross: We've won! We've won _____!

Individual speaking

Think about things that you had to last week, have to this week, or will have to do next week. These pictures may help to give you some ideas.

   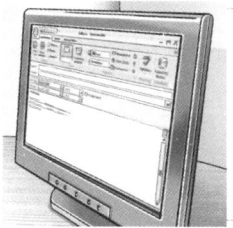 

2 Make notes. Use your own ideas, too.

Last week	This week	Next week

3 Write sentences about the things you had to, have to and will have to do.

4 Talk about all the things that you had to do last week, have to do this week and will have to do next week.

Check-out 12

Reading

1. You read a scene from a playscript. a What did the children often go to see? _____
   b What happened to the railway line at the beginning? _____
2. a How many characters were in the scene? _____
   b Where was the scene set? _____

Vocabulary

1. You learned 20 words to do with a disaster. Look at page 125 in this book.
   Do you know what all these words mean? Check any that you are not sure of in your dictionary.
2. Decide whether these phrases tell you the time when something happened, the place it happened or how it happened. Write *time*, *place* or *how* after each phrase.
   a on Monday afternoon _____ b in the kitchen _____ c slowly and carefully _____
3. Write the adjective ending *-ive*: a Sunglasses protect. They are _____.
   b Flowers attract insects. Flowers are _____ to them.
4. Write words beginning *wa-* for these meanings:
   a a fighter in an army _____   b to walk slowly and without direction _____
   c to float gently in the air _____

Grammar

1. Complete the sentence in the second conditional:

   If we _____ (have) some moncy, we _____ (buy) mum some flowers.

   Mum _____ (be) very happy if we _____ (buy) her some flowers.
2. Complete: I _____ go now! My bus is coming soon and I _____ miss it.
3. Underline the correct phrase: The bus *broke out / broke off / broke down*, so everyone had to get off.

Writing

1. Complete these features of a playscript:

   The names of the character are on the _____ side of the page. The words the characters say come after their _____. The playscript does not use s_____ m_____. The s_____ d_____ tell the characters what to do and how to speak.
2. Have you made a neat copy of your playscript? ☐   Is it in your folder? ☐

Listening and speaking

1. Have you listened again to Laura and Ross talking about the things they have to do? ☐
2. Did your friend ask you what you have to do this week? ☐
3. Did you ask your friend? ☐
4. Have you talked for one minute about things you have to do in the next few weeks? ☐

Check-out 12 complete ☐

Revision 6 (Units 11 and 12)

1 Re-write the sentences as reported speech. Change the tenses of the verbs and make any other necessary changes.

1 "Flynn is the new owner of the club," a man explained.
_____

2 "I usually travel by car," said Mr Flynn.
_____

3 "We're enjoying the match," the fans said.
_____

4 The goalkeeper said, "We're playing well at the moment."
_____

5 "We'll win every match," the players promised.
_____

2 Complete the sentences with one of the words in brackets.

1 Drivers _____ use the ring road get to work quicker. (which / who)

2 We try not to travel at rush hour _____ the streets are very busy. (when / that)

3 Cyclists like the cycle lanes _____ cars and buses are banned. (which / where)

4 The streets _____ used to be polluted are now much cleaner. (which / where)

5 The "Park and ride" scheme _____ started last year has been a success. (who / that)

3 Complete the sentences with the correct form of the verbs in brackets. These sentences practise the second conditional.

1 There isn't a train on the line but if a train _____ along now, it _____ into the mound of earth. (come, crash)

2 The station isn't close by. The children _____ there if it _____ not so far away. (run, be)

3 They haven't got any red flags but if they _____ red flags, they _____ warn the train driver. (have, be able to)

4 Lucy doesn't sing very well. If she _____ better, she _____ join the choir. (sing, can)

5 Billy always fails his science exam. He _____ the exam if he _____ harder. (pass, study)

4 Write the words in the correct order.

1 hard to students project. had work their have The on _____

2 the Laura to videos. had edit _____

3 work. their to Today check have they _____

4 must copy. to a remember They make _____

5 have entry will soon. post their They to _____

5 Complete the sentences with the words in the box. Make any necessary changes.

| clumsy | weird | disaster | top speed | skilful | deliberately |
| relax | shocked | slip | accident | manager | lead |

1 Joe didn't break the glass _____. He's just a very _____ boy.
2 The _____ chose his most _____ players to be in the team.
3 Unfortunately when United took the _____, they _____ and let their opponents score.
4 "You have all failed your exams," said the teacher in a _____ voice. "This is a complete _____."
5 The police drove at _____ to the scene of the _____.
6 As the mud and earth _____ down the hill, it made a _____ noise.

6 Make compound nouns by joining words from both boxes.

| sun | rail | eye | skate |
| goal | business | cross | air |

| brow | board | port | man |
| roads | light | keeper | way |

1 _____ 2 _____ 3 _____ 4 _____
5 _____ 6 _____ 7 _____ 8 _____

7 Complete the sentences with the verbs in the boxes. Use the correct form!

| make | do | break |

1 Why have we stopped? _____ the car _____ down?
2 When they baked a cake, the children _____ an awful mess in the kitchen.
3 You can _____ all your shopping at the shopping centre.
4 Thieves _____ into the museum last night.
5 Can someone help me _____ the dishes, please?
6 If you cancel her party, Jemima _____ a terrible fuss.

Grammar reference

Present simple See Unit 1

We use the present simple for things that happen regularly.

We go to the seaside every summer.   *Joe watches TV every day.*

There are some verbs which are normally only used in the simple form.

I know that man.

e.g. like, love, hate, want, understand, remember, need, prefer, know, mean, sound, think (have an opinion), have (possession).

Affirmative	I/You/We/They + verb	They take exams once a year.
	He/She/It + verb + s (or es)	John plays football every day.
		Sara goes to school by bus.
Negative	I/You/We/They + do not + verb	I do not like cold weather.
	He/She/It + does not + verb	It does not snow in August.
Interrogative	Do + I/you/we/they + verb + ?	Do you speak French?
	Does + he/she/it + verb + ?	Does she live in London?
Short answers	Yes, I/you/we/they + do. No, I/you/we/they + don't.	Yes, we do. No, they don't.
	Yes, he/she/it + does. No, he/she/it + doesn't.	Yes, he does. No, it doesn't.

Present continuous See Units 1 and 3

1) We use the present continuous for things that are happening now.

   At the moment Sam is watching his favourite TV programme.
   The students are writing their essays now.

2) We can use the present continuous for future events which are the result of plans/arrangements in the present.

   We're having pizza for dinner tonight.
   My cousins are coming to stay next weekend.
   Harry is taking his driving test next week.

Affirmative	I am + verb + ing.	I am studying at the moment.
	You/We/They are + verb + ing.	They are sleeping now.
	He/She/It is + verb + ing.	Look! It is raining.
Negative	I am not + verb + ing.	I am not listening.
	You/We/They are not + verb + ing.	We are not sleeping.
	He/She/It is not + verb + ing.	He is not watching TV.
Interrogative	Am I + verb + ing + ?	Am I dreaming?
	Are you/we/they + verb + ing + ?	Are they sleeping?
	Is he/she/it + verb + ing + ?	Is Joe coming?
Short answers	Yes, I am. No, I'm not.	
	Yes, you/we/they + are.	No, you/we/they + aren't.
		No, you're/we're/they're + not.
	Yes, he/she/it + is.	No, he/she/it + isn't.
		No, he's/she's/it's + not.
	Yes, we are. No, we aren't.	No, we're not.
	Yes, he is. No, he isn't.	No, he's not.

Past simple   See Unit 2

We use the past simple for actions which were completed in the past.
> *Philippe entered the square.*
> *When Philippe saw the man, he became suspicious.*

Affirmative	I/You/He/She/It/We/They + verb + ed (regular verbs) + past simple (irregular verbs) *Jill passed her exams. We went to the shopping centre.*
Negative	I/You/He/She/It/We/They + did not + verb *I did not buy a new camera.*
Interrogative	Did + I/you/he/she/it/we/ they + verb + ? *Did you enjoy the film?*
Short answers	Yes, I/you/he/she/it/we/they + did. No, I/you/he/she/it/we/they + didn't. *Yes, she did. No, they didn't.*

Past continuous   See Unit 2

We use the past continuous for actions which continued for some time in the past.
> *The man was taking photos.*

Affirmative	I/He/She/It + was + verb + ing. *The child was crying.* You/We/They + were + verb + ing. *The boys were shouting.*
Negative	I/He/She/It + was not + verb + ing. *The man was not smiling.* You/We/They + were not + verb + ing. *The girls were not singing.*
Interrogative	Was + I/he/she/it + verb + ing + ? *Was she laughing?* Were + you/we/they + verb + ing + ? *Were you sleeping?*

Short answers	Yes, I/he/she/it + was. No, I/he/she/it + wasn't.
	     Yes, she was. No, he wasn't.
	 Yes, you/we/they + were. No, you/we/they + weren't.
	     Yes, we were. No, they weren't.

Past simple and past continuous   See Unit 2

You can use both tenses in one sentence when a short, sudden action interrupts a longer, continuing action. Use *while* or *when*.
> *While Joe was watching TV, the telephone rang.*
> *Joe was watching TV when the telephone rang.*

Used to   See Unit 2

We use *used to* for actions which
1) happened regularly in the past but not now.
   Joe used to walk to school but now he goes by bus.
2) continued for some time in the past but not now.
   Joe used to like football but now he prefers basketball.

Affirmative	I/You/He/She/It/We/They + used to + verb
	He used to have a fast car.
Negative	I/You/He/She/It/We/They + did not + use to + verb
	She did not use to study hard.
Interrogative	Did + I/you/he/she/it/we/they + use to + verb + ?
	Did they use to live in London?
Short answers	Yes, I/you/he/she/it/we/they + did. No, I/you/he/she/it/we/they + didn't.
	Yes, I did. No, we didn't.

Future simple   See Unit 3

We use *will* + verb for actions which will happen in the future.

The concert will take place on Saturday.

Affirmative	I/You/He/She/It/We/They + will + verb
	The shops will open in an hour.
Negative	I/You/He/She/It/We/They + will not + verb
	The train will not arrive on time.
Interrogative	Will + I/you/he/she/it/we/they + verb + ?
	Will you pass your exams?
Short answers	Yes, I/you/he/she/it/we/they + will. No, I/you/he/she/it/we/they + won't.
	Yes, it will. No, she won't.

Be going to   See Unit 3

We use *be going to* + verb

1) when talking about plans and intentions.
    John is going to be a doctor.
2) when a situation in the present means that an action is sure to happen in the future.
    Look at those black clouds! It's going to rain.

Affirmative	I am + going to + verb	I am going to miss the train.
	You/We/They are + going to + verb	We are going to watch TV.
	He/She/It is + going to + verb	Jane is going to buy a new dress.
Negative	I am not + going to + verb	I am not going to watch the match.
	You/We/They are not + going to + verb	They are not going to play.
	He/She/It is not + going to + verb	It is not going to snow.
Interrogative	Am I + going to + verb + ?	Am I going to be scared?
	Are you/we/they + going to + verb + ?	Are you going to read this book?
	Is he/she/it + going to + verb + ?	Is Sam going to pass his exams?
Short answers	Yes, I am.	No, I'm not.	
	Yes, you/we/they are.	No, we/you/they aren't.	No, we're/you're/they're not.
	Yes, you are.	No, you aren't.	No, you're not.
	Yes, he/she/it is.	No, he/she/it isn't.	No, he's/she's/it's not.
	Yes, he is.	No, he isn't.	No, he's not.

Present perfect simple   See Units 4 and 10

We use the present perfect simple

1) for actions that have happened during a period of time leading up to the present. Exactly when the actions happened is unknown or unimportant.

   Miranda and Jason have tried many sports.

2) when an action happened in the past and we can see the result of that action now.

   Look! Someone has broken the window.

3) for states or actions which started in the past and still continue now.
   Use *since* + a definite time.   *My uncle has lived in Paris since 2005.*
   Use *for* + a period of time.   *Sally has been ill for two weeks.*

4) with *just* for actions which happened a very short time ago.

   Harry has just gone to school.

5) with *yet* in questions and negative sentences.

   Have you finished your homework yet?
   I haven't written my composition yet.

6) for actions that happened at an indefinite time in the past.

   My uncle has been to China.

7) with *ever* and *never*.

   Have you ever seen a tiger?
   She hasn't ever been abroad.
   She has never been abroad.

Affirmative	I/You/We/They + have + past participle	I have been to Spain.
	He/She/It + has + past participle	He has played in the team.
Negative	I/You/We/They + have not + past participle	They have not finished their work.
	He/She/It + has not + past participle	It has not rained for months.
Interrogative	Have I/you/we/they + past participle + ?	Have you eaten your lunch?
	Has he/she/it + past participle + ?	Has the plane landed yet?
Short answers	Yes, I/you/we/they have. No, I/you/we/they haven't. Yes, we have. No, they haven't. Yes, he/she/it has. No, he/she/it hasn't. Yes, he has. No, she hasn't.	

Present perfect continuous   See Unit 10

We use the present perfect continuous

1) when an action started in the past and is still continuing now.

   Lisa has been talking on the phone for hours.

   We often use a time phrase to show how long the action has been continuing:

   ... since 3 o'clock.   ... for a long time.

2) when the result of a past action is visible now and that action continued for some time.

   Meg's eyes are red. I think she's been crying.

Affirmative	I/You/We/They + have + been + verb + ing	They have been playing tennis.
	He/She/It + has + been + verb + ing	It has been raining.
Negative	I/You/We/They + have + not + been + verb + ing	I have not been studying.
	He/She/It + has + not + been + verb + ing	Joe has not been swimming.
Interrogative	Have + I/you/we/they + been + verb + ing + ?	Have you been sleeping?
	Has + he/she/it + been + verb + ing + ?	Has she been crying?
Short answers	Yes, I/you/we/they have. No, I/you/we/they haven't.	
	Yes, we have. No, they haven't.	
	Yes, he/she/it has. No, he/she/it hasn't.	
	Yes, he has. No, she hasn't.	

Conditional sentences   See Units 7, 8 and 12

1) In **zero conditional** sentences we use the present tense in both clauses when we are talking about general truths and scientific facts.

> *If the temperature drops below zero, water freezes.*
> *Ice melts if the temperature rises above zero.*

2) In **first conditional** sentences we are thinking about the future.
Use the future tense in the main clause.
Use the present tense in the *if* clause.

> *We will go to the beach tomorrow if the weather is fine.*
> *If you go to New York, you will see lots of skyscrapers.*

Unless means *if not*.

> *If Joe doesn't work harder, he will fail his exams.*
> *Unless Joe works harder, he will fail his exams.*
> *I won't go to the party if you don't go with me.*
> *I won't go to the party unless you go with me.*

3) In **second conditional** sentences we are talking about the present time.

> *I haven't got a lot of money.*
> *If I had a lot of money, I would travel round the world.*
> *I live in apartment.*
> *If I lived in a house with a garden, I would get a dog.*

Use the past tense after *if*. Use *would* + verb in the main clause.

In the main clause *would be able to* can be replaced by *could*.

> *If he went to China, he would be able to learn Chinese.*
> *If he went to China, he could learn Chinese.*

Reported speech   See Unit 11

In reported speech
- when the reporting verb is the past (*He said that ..., She told me that ..., A man shouted that ...*) the verbs which were in the direct speech often change.

1) Present tenses becomes past tenses:

"The watch is expensive."	He said that the watch was expensive.
"The dog is barking."	He said that the dog was barking.
"The boys walk to school."	He said that the boys walked to school.

2) *will* becomes *would*:
   "The exams will be hard."   He said that the exams would be hard.
   "Not everyone will pass."   He said that not everyone would pass.
- subject pronouns can change.
   "I am ill," he said.   He said that he was ill.
   "You are late," he told me.   He told me that I was late.
   "You are early," he told the girl. He told the girl that she was early.

Always think of the meaning of the sentences and you won't go wrong!

Modal verbs   See Unit 8

Meanings of the modal verbs (*may, might, can, could, should, ought to, must*)

may:	possibility	It may rain this afternoon.
	permission (polite)	May I bring a friend to the party?
might:	possibility	We might go to America next year.
can:	ability	Jane can sing beautifully.
	permission	You can stay up to watch the film.
could:	ability (in the past)	He could speak French fluently when he was a boy.
	permission (polite)	Could I borrow your dictionary, please?
should:	obligation	You should clean those dirty shoes.
ought to:	obligation	John ought to work harder.
must:	obligation	We must always be polite.
	necessity	You must get to the airport by 10 o'clock.

Affirmative	subject + modal verb + infinitive without *to* (except *ought to*)
	It might rain. He can speak Chinese. You ought to leave.
Negative	subject + modal verb + *not* + infinitive without *to* (except *ought to*)
	She could not swim. We may not like the film. He ought not to shout.
Interrogative	modal verb + subject + infinitive without *to* (except *ought to*) + ?
	Must we take a test? Should I buy that book? Ought you to do that?
Short answers	Yes, + subject + modal verb. No, + subject + modal verb + *not* (short form)
	Yes, we can. No, they mustn't.
Passive	subject + modal verb + passive infinitive without *to* (except *ought to*)
	A bridge should be built. The questions must be answered.
	The treasure cannot be found. That tree ought to be cut down.

Have to and Must   See Unit 12

In affirmative sentences *have to* and *must* have the same meaning:
   You have to work hard.   You must work hard.
   (It is necessary to work hard. You have an obligation to work hard.)

In questions *have to* and *must* have the same meaning:
   Do you have to go?   Must you go?

In negative sentences *have to* and *must* have different meanings:
   You do not have to leave now. (It is not necessary to leave now.)
   You must not leave now. (You are forbidden to leave now.)

Passive See Unit 9

1) We use the passive when:
   - we do not know who does the action
   - we do not care who does the action
   - we know who does the action but we do not want to say.

   Dad's car was stolen.   *The painting will be sold.*   *A window has been broken.*

2) We also use the passive when the person or thing that does the action is important or significant.

   The competition was won by a student from our school.
   The town has been damaged by a violent storm.

Present:	subject + am/is/are + past participle	Rice is grown in India.
Past:	subject + was/were + past participle	Trees were blown down by the storm.
Future:	subject + will + be + past participle	New houses will be built on this land.
Present perfect:	subject + have/has + been + past participle	The tree has been cut down.

Verbs + infinitive or gerund See Unit 6

Some verbs are followed by the infinitive.

   Sally is planning to do a design course.

need, want, plan, help, decide, manage + infinitive

Some verbs are followed by the gerund.

   She doesn't mind working hard.

like, hate, enjoy, mind, look forward to, be good/bad at, be interested in + gerund

Question tags See Unit 9

When the sentence is negative, the question tag is affirmative.

   The shops aren't open, are they?

When the sentence is affirmative, the question tag is negative.

   The lady is selling honey, isn't she?

We use auxiliary verbs + pronouns in question tags:

   I'm wrong, aren't I?   *You speak Spanish, don't you?*
   You aren't angry, are you?   *They don't eat meat, do they?*
   They're sleeping, aren't they?   *He plays basketball, doesn't he?*
   She's playing tennis, isn't she?   *I'm not running, am I?*
   It isn't cold today, is it?   *She doesn't live in the city, does she?*
   He's not studying, is he?

Articles See Unit 6

1) When we talk about something for the first time, we use *a* or *an*.
   When we mention it again, we use *the*.

   He saw a horse and a cow. The horse was black. The cow was white.

2) We use *the* when we know there is only one of something.

   George knocked on the door.

3) With plural nouns and uncountable nouns we use no article when we are speaking in general. When we are speaking about something specific, we use *the*.

   I like strawberries but the strawberries that I bought aren't sweet.
   We can't live without water. The water in our river is polluted.

Comparative adjectives See Unit 5

When you compare two items
- if they are the same, use *as ... as*.
  Lily is as tall as her brother.
- if they are different, use *-er than* or *more ... than*.
  Ben is older than his sister.   *Anna is more intelligent than Ben.*

Use *-er than* with
- one-syllable adjectives: *big, small*
- some two-syllable adjectives: *noisy, busy, quiet*

Use *more ... than* with
- some two-syllable adjectives: *peaceful, harmless*
- adjectives with three or more syllables: *dangerous, complicated, interesting*

Superlative adjectives See Unit 5

Superlative adjectives have two forms:
- *the* adjective + *est*: *January is the coldest month.*
- *the most* + adjective: *This is the most delicious cake.*

Use *the* adjective + *est* with
- one-syllable adjectives: *hot, tall*
- some two-syllable adjectives: *heavy, lazy, clever*

Use the *most* + adjective with
- some two-syllable adjectives: *polite, handsome*
- adjectives with three syllables or more: *beautiful, astonishing*

Don't forget the irregular adjectives: *good, better, the best*   *bad, worse, the worst*

Some, any, much, many, a little, a few, a lot of See Unit 7

With countable nouns we use *some, any, many, a few*.
  There are some cars in the street. There aren't any lorries.
  There are so many people! There are only a few children.

With uncountable nouns we use *some, any, much, a little*.
  There is some water in the jug. There isn't any juice.
  How much food have we got? We've got a little meat.

We use *lots of* and *a lot of* with countable and uncountable nouns.
  There are lots of shops. OR *There are a lot of shops.*
  There is lots of time. OR *There is a lot of time.*

We usually use *any* in questions. *Have you got any money?*
We always use *any* in negative sentences. *I haven't got any pets.*

Relative clauses See Unit 11

In relative clauses you can use
- *which* or *that* to refer to things or animals.
  The film which I saw was great.   This is the fish that I caught.
- *who* or *that* to refer to people.
  That's the boy who found the ring.   The man that bought the house is French.
- *where* to refer to a place and *when* to refer to a time.
  This is the town where I was born. August is the month when we go on holiday.

Irregular verb list

Infinitive	Past simple	Past participle	Infinitive	Past simple	Past participle
be	was	been	grow	grew	grown
beat	beat	beaten	hang	hung	hung
become	became	become	have	had	had
begin	began	begun	hear	heard	heard
bet	bet	bet	hide	hid	hidden
bite	bit	bitten	hold	held	held
blow	blew	blown	hurt	hurt	hurt
break	broke	broken	keep	kept	kept
bring	brought	brought	kneel	knelt*	knelt*
build	built	built	know	knew	known
burn	burnt*	burnt*	lay	laid	laid
burst	burst	burst	lead	led	led
buy	bought	bought	lean	leant*	leant*
catch	caught	caught	leap	leapt*	leapt*
choose	chose	chosen	learn	learnt*	learnt*
come	came	come	leave	left	left
cost	cost	cost	lend	lent	lent
cut	cut	cut	let	let	let
dig	dug	dug	lie	lay	lain
do	did	done	light	lit	lit
draw	drew	drawn	lose	lost	lost
dream	dreamt*	dreamt*	make	made	made
drink	drank	drunk	mean	meant	meant
drive	drove	driven	meet	met	met
eat	ate	eaten	pay	paid	paid
fall	fell	fallen	put	put	put
feed	fed	fed	read	read	read
feel	felt	felt	ride	rode	ridden
fight	fought	fought	ring	rang	rung
find	found	found	rise	rose	risen
fly	flew	flown	run	ran	run
forget	forgot	forgotten	say	said	said
freeze	froze	frozen	see	saw	seen
give	gave	given	sell	sold	sold
get	got	got	send	sent	sent
go	went	gone	set	set	set

Irregular verb list

Infinitive	Past simple	Past participle
shake	shook	shaken
shine	shone	shone
shoot	shot	shot
show	showed	shown*
shut	shut	shut
sing	sang	sung
sink	sank	sunk
sit	sat	sat
sleep	slept	slept
slide	slid	slid
smell	smelt*	smelt*
speak	spoke	spoken
speed	sped	sped
spend	spent	spent
spill	spilt*	spilt*
spin	spun	spun
split	split	split
spread	spread	spread
stand	stood	stood
steal	stole	stolen
stick	stuck	stuck
swim	swam	swum
swing	swung	swung
take	took	taken
teach	taught	taught
tear	tore	torn
tell	told	told
think	thought	thought
throw	threw	thrown
understand	understood	understood
wake	woke	woken
wear	wore	worn
weave	wove	woven
win	won	won
write	wrote	written

Verbs marked * also have regular forms:
burn, burned, burned; dream, dreamed, dreamed; learn, learned, learned, etc.

Word list

Unit 1
Words to do with working on a group project
construct
create
decide
discuss
enthusiastic
excitement
get on (progress)
imagination
include
invite
popular
present v
produce
respond
response
run (organise)
session
subject
surf v (internet)
volunteer n / v

buzz
chance n
evidently
limit n
local
motivate
neighbourhood
portrait
rush n
technology

words ending -*tion*
animation
construction
creation
invitation
motivation
presentation
production

words ending -*ssion*
discussion
impression
mission
procession

Unit 2
Words used in describing a city square
broad
bustling
disguise
drift
dusty
elegant
entrance
fume
gallop
glisten
hiss
mingle
movement
oily
particularly
recognise
scent
shade
spot (see)
take notice

cascade
chariot
click
coo
cruise
dart v
duke
frown
gape
never-ending
no longer
pigeon
snack
spurt
startle
strut

spelling
cancel
quarrel
refer

Unit 3
Words to do with animals, habitat and threats
appearance
ban
climate
diet
extinct
female
habitat
industry
male
newborn
pollution
region
reproduction
seal
shore
snowdrift
spill
survive
threaten
whiskers

alert
bob
chest
den
entire
floe
fully
guarantee
harmful
insulate
mammal
partly
patiently
polar
prey
pup
seize
tanker

uncertain
waterproof

words ending -*al*
coastal
comical
continual
electrical
factual
final
industrial
internal
musical
natural
normal
seasonal
several

words ending -*y*
dirty
dusty
furry
handy
nutty
powdery
smoky
starry

ei / *ie* words
grief
receive
seize

Unit 4
Words to do with advertising an adventure sports centre
automatic
booking n
challenge
confident
contact
electrifying
entry
exhilarating
half price
indoor
membership

provide
qualified
reduction
runway
skills
swoop
trainer (person)
unforgettable
unique

aerial
benefit
bird's eye view
bungee jump
complex n
members-only
off
selected
sky-diving
suspended
unmissable
vertical

words ending -ent / -ence
confidence
difference
evidence
evident
excellence
obedience
patience
silence

words ending -ant / -ance
brilliance
defiance
elegance
ignorance
importance
reliance

Unit 5
Words to do with the life events of a ruler
adore
allow
condition
devastated
exhausting
expand
expansion
harsh
immensely
lonely
period
population
progress
public
rather
refuse
rely on
remove
share
strict

childhood
duty
governess
guidance
handsome
matter
prime minister
request
role
ruler
sadden
state
support
tutor
wedding

words ending -ment
agreement
announcement
appointment
argument
arrangement
disappointment
entertainment
equipment
excitement
government
measurement
movement
payment
statement

words with gu
guilty

Unit 6
Words describing a person's appearance and craftsman's tools
cheek
cheeky
cheerful
concentration
droop
expression
eyebrow
fashion (way)
forehead
glimpse
grin
moustache
penknife
screwdriver
sharpen
sharp-eyed
striking
tools
waft
workbench

ascend
carve
crescent
crimson
descend
intricately
laden
lean v
mind v
perch
pliers
rim
rosy
satisfaction
scrutinise
simmer
tasty
varnish
workshop

words ending -ate
celebrate
concentrate
delicate
educate
fascinate
fortunate
illustrate
insulate
intricate
separate

Unit 7
Words for ingredients and cooking
beat
beefburgers
chop
crush
filling
finely
form v
fresh
freshly
fridge
fry
get out

123

ground pepper
herb
ingredients
medium
prepare
refrigerate
roll (bread)
sauce

clove
fall apart
garlic
mayonnaise
minced beef
olive oil
parsley
thyme
tomato ketchup

words with prefix *pre-*
precede
predict
preheat
preview

words ending *-ture*
culture
furniture
future
sculpture

Unit 8
Words to do with animals in captivity
abolish
ban
behaviour
boredom
captivity
continual
convince
cruel
disgrace
existence
exploitation
instincts
isolation
post v (put up)

precisely
prison
regular
stress
suffer
unbelievably

according
available
close-up
exchange
link
occupy
pace
pant
pound
related
update

words with prefix *im-*
impatient
imperfect
impolite
improbable

words with prefix *in-*
incredible
independent
indirect
informal
inseparable
invisible

homophones
source
role
mail

words with *ci / ti*
cautious
initial
official
optician

Unit 9
Words to do with the eye and sight
approximately
automatically
blink
brain
detect
eyelash
eyelid
focus
goggles
human
iris
movie
muscle
nerve
pupil
purpose
tough
transparent
upper
vision

baseball
cornea
lens
optic
ouch
sclera
visor
weld

words ending *-ible*
credible
divisible
horrible
sensible
visible

words ending *-able*
believable
breakable
likeable
lovable
noticeable
separable

words ending *-sion*
confusion
decision
inclusion
vision

Unit 10
Words to do with behaviour and feelings
cheerfully
cheerfulness
come round (visit)
concentrate
concerned
depressed
embarrass
enquire
glance
inspire
miss
modestly
occasion
opportunity
pause
regain
suggest
suggestion
talent
tremendous

album
biological
breeze
certainty
chemistry
cheque
crisp
enquiringly
gallery
grade
plenty
radiant
shimmering
text book
translucent
ultimately

words ending -ous
courageous
famous
furious
glorious
gorgeous
marvellous
nervous
ridiculous
various

Unit 11
Words to do with football
clumsy
dodge
equalise
fan
foul
goalkeeper
half-time
header
kick-off
manager
opponent
pass
reserve
semi-final
show-off
skilful
splendid
swift
tackle
wing

address (speak to)
chauffeur-driven
cross
deliberate
execute
first-class
fixtures list
flag v
forward n
invest
jubilant
justify
lead
limousine
long-time
power v
predictable
ragged
relax
release
roller skates
soar
spot n
staff
striker
stunt
substitute
turn up

compound nouns
airline
businessman
crossroads
workbench

words with -tch-
pitcher
satchel

Unit 12
Words to do with a railway
disaster
accident
brainwave
bush
danger
desperately
disaster
familiar
firm
landslide
like mad
massive
mound
reach
shocked
situation
slip
terrible
top speed
urgently
weird

flagpole
flannel
petticoat
telegraph

words ending -ive
active
attractive
impressive
possessive
protective

words with a after w
sounding o
waft
wander

Conversational words and phrases

Absolutely!	A: The trip to London was fantastic, wasn't it? B: Absolutely! I loved it.
Actually	A: Have you ever been to Italy? B: Well, actually, I went there last summer.
All right	A: Shall we go shopping tomorrow afternoon? B: All right. I'll meet you at three.
Any ideas?	We ought to get a birthday present for Grandma. Any ideas?
Certainly not!	A: Mum, can I have a pony for my birthday? B: Certainly not! A pony's much too expensive.
Congratulations!	A: I won a gold medal at the swimming competition. B: Congratulations!
Definitely!	A: Are you going to Molly's party? B: Definitely! She always has fantastic parties.
Don't speak too soon!	A: I'm sure we'll get to the airport in time. B: Don't speak too soon! We're not there yet.
Exactly!	A: The old swimming pool is really horrible. B: Exactly! This town needs a new sports centre.
Good idea!	A: Let's buy Mum some earrings for her birthday. B: Good idea!
Good thinking!	A: If we go by car, we'll get to the match on time. B: Good thinking! I'll ask Dad to drive us there.
Gosh!	A: Look at this amazing guitar. B: Gosh! It's so expensive!
Guess what!	Guess what! The president is visiting our town next week!
Here goes …	I've never done a bungee jump before. It's terrifying! Here goes … Aghhhh!
Here he is / they are, etc.	Has Jon arrived yet? Oh, here he is!
Here we are!	Here we are! We've arrived at last!
Hey!	Hey! Stop! That's not your suitcase. It's mine.
Hi there!	A: Hi there, Sally! B: Oh! Hello!
Hmm …	A: What do you think of our new science teacher? B: Hmm … I'm not sure.
How / What about you?	I'm looking forward to the holidays. How about you?
I bet	A: I'm going to Paris next weekend. B: Really? I bet you can't wait!
I can't wait!	Only two weeks till the holidays. I can't wait!
I get it	Why are you grinning? Oh, I get it! You passed your exam!

I'm afraid	I'm afraid I can't come to your party on Saturday. Sorry!
I'm deadly serious	A: Are you joking? B: No, I'm deadly serious.
Let me see ...	A: My pen's not working. Have you got a spare one? B: Let me see ... Yes, here you are!
Lucky you / him / her, etc!	You're going on a trip to New York? Lucky you!
Me, too	A: I've got loads of homework this evening. B: Me, too.
... my kind of thing	A: Do you like skiing? B: No. Winter sports aren't my kind of thing.
Never mind	A: I've left my textbook at home. B: Never mind. You can share mine.
Not at all	A: Thanks for your help. B: Not at all.
Of course!	A: It's Mum's birthday next week. Shall we get her a present? B: Of course!
Off you go!	Are you ready to start your presentation? OK, off you go!
Oh, dear!	A: I got a terrible mark in my maths exam. B: Oh, dear! Can you take it again?
OK	A: Let's go to the beach. B: OK. I'll bring a picnic.
Oops!	The path is really icy. Oops! I nearly fell.
... or what?	Look at that sports car! Fantastic or what?
Poor you / him / her, etc!	You've broken your leg? Oh, poor you!
Really?	A: I've been made captain of the basketball team. B: Really? That's fantastic!
See you later!	A: Bye! B: Bye! See you later!
So ...	So ... what do you think of our new teacher?
Sorry!	Did I step on your foot? Sorry!
Stop making (Don't make) such a fuss!	Your shoes look fine and your dress isn't awful at all. Stop making such a fuss!
Thank goodness (for that)!	A: The climbers have been rescued from the mountain. B: Thank goodness!
Thanks a lot	It's a wonderful present. Thanks a lot.
That's awesome!	You won first prize? Wow! That's awesome!

That's right	A: Are you from Spain? B: Yes, that's right.
To be honest	A: What did you think of the exam? B: To be honest, I found it really difficult.
Ugh!	Ugh! This fruit juice tastes disgusting.
Wait a minute!	That's a nice jacket you're wearing. Wait a minute! It's my jacket!
Well, ...	A: What did you think of the film? B: Well, it wasn't bad, I suppose.
Well done!	A: I got 98 per cent in my exam. B: That's great! Well done!
What a mess!	Jack hasn't tidied his room for weeks. What a mess!
What a nightmare!	We had to wait at the airport for 48 hours. What a nightmare!
What else?	So you're studying English and French. What else?
What on earth ...?	Look at that boy. What on earth is he doing?
What's the matter?	You look miserable. What's the matter?
Who knows?	Will Holly become a famous fashion designer? Who knows?
Wow!	A: The volcano's starting to erupt. B: Wow! It's amazing!
You know	Have you met Brad yet? You know, the boy from Canada.
You mean ...	A: We're going to Australia. B: You mean, you're going to live there?
You're / You've got to be joking!	A: I've just seen an elephant in the garden. B: You're joking!
You, too	A: Have a good weekend! B: Thanks. You, too!
Yum!	Yum! This strawberry ice cream is delicious!